Working with
TRUCKS and BUSES

DAVID J. LEEMING
HNC (Mech Eng), LCG, FIMI, MIRTE, MBIM

Batsford Academic and Educational Limited *London*

To my daughter Beverley
wishing her every success
in her choice of career

Filmset by Progress Filmsetting Limited, London EC2

Printed and bound in Great Britain by
Redwood Burn Limited, Trowbridge and Esher
for the publishers
Batsford Academic and Educational Limited
an imprint of B. T. Batsford Ltd.
4 Fitzhardinge Street, London W1H 0AH

Contents

4

Acknowledgment to plates between pages 72 and 73

Final adjustments are carried out at the end of the line to ensure the vehicle can go into immediate service

Wheel fitting is now an automatic and efficient operation

Fitting a ten-speed gear box behind a 280 hsp 6 cylinder turbocharged diesel engine

'Flatting-down' a body panel before painting

Vehicle testing on a computerised rolling road ensures accurate and consistent results

Replacing a wheel on a modern double-deck bus

Working conditions in a modern bus service bay are designed to provide a clean, safe and efficient environment

The above seven are photographs by Roger Brown and all are reproduced by kind permission of Leyland Vehicles Limited.

Vehicle passing through water splash to cool dampness following rough road testing
Photograph by Rodney Barnes

Gearbox test rig
Photograph by Denis Gibbons

General view of a test track
Photograph by Roger Brown

Vehicle on high speed circuit on which a hands-off start can be achieved when vehicle reaches 70 mph
Photograph by Rodney Barnes

The author would like to thank the professional and examination bodies, the trade associations and trade unions, and the various companies in the truck and bus industry who have so willingly furnished information about their organisations to make this book informative to readers.

Your choice of career

The First Step

Selecting a career is a difficult task for most young people as it means making a decision. Even though you will have to make many more decisions during your life there may never be another one quite as important apart from, perhaps, your life partner. Plenty of time and much thought must be given before the final decision on your career is reached and this means you will have to do a good deal of reading, asking many questions, and exploring many different avenues. Don't hesitate to ask your parents or guardian for their advice as they themselves have had to take the same step during their life, and their experiences which led to their decision will no doubt be of value to you.

The career you choose will affect your whole life, your health and happiness, and it is going to occupy a considerable proportion of your life right up to the time you retire. The lack of ample consideration before making your decision increases the risk of making a wrong choice of career and this often leads to unhappiness and misery which will make you regret your decision for many years ahead.

There are a few young people, and you may know one or two, who think they know what they want to do for a career at the age of 14 or earlier because they feel that they have a natural ability and interest to go into a particular job. But there are far more who have no idea what they want to do and some of them find it hard, if not agonising, to make their decision.

Before you make your decision it is worth bearing in mind that you are going to spend about one-third of your working days at your place of work and this commitment is likely to last up to the age of 60 or beyond so it is well worth taking a little time and trouble to explore the opportunities open to you. If you do make the right choice your career will no doubt be interesting and rewarding, as well as remunerative, and you are far more likely to live a happy and contented life.

A career with trucks and buses

If you are considering a job which involves trucks and buses your first step is to gather as much information as possible on the truck and bus industry. You may obtain this information by talking to people, reading leaflets, magazines and books, watching relevant television programmes, and seeking advice from people who are able to give a professional service. After receiving advice and information on the truck and bus industry you should not hesitate to let your parents know if you find this industry interesting so that you can be given the best possible guidance right from the beginning.

Don't forget that there are careers teachers in schools who are willing to see pupils and advise them on their future careers. Careers teachers are usually selected to do this work because they have an interest in industry and commerce and they have leaflets and charts on a wide range of careers which should include the truck and bus industry.

Each local education authority has a team of careers officers professionally trained to help young people who are seeking a career. You should take advantage of your careers officer by contacting him (or her) for further guidance and advice on your proposed career which may well lead to an interview, arranged by the officer, with a company in the truck and bus industry. Your careers officer is concerned with the placement of young people into jobs and once fixed up he is further concerned in providing a follow-up service and further vocational guidance for young people who require this. His well established links with companies enable him to acquire information on jobs and job prospects easily and quickly and his experience in seeking information of a specialised nature through the library services can also be of use to you. It is a good idea to take your parents with you when you go along to see your careers officer so that you all hear his advice and this enables you all to put questions to him during the interview and discuss between yourselves afterwards the points he makes.

Careers conventions and exhibitions are periodically held in schools,

8

colleges and other local authority buildings where you can go along and talk to careers officers, college lecturers, company training officers, industrial training board advisers, and many other people who can offer advice and information on careers and jobs.

One of the many advantages of attending a careers convention is the opportunity of being able to see demonstrations of skills used in particular industries, in addition to benefiting from advice and literature which is freely available. Models of vehicles and components, wall charts showing careers, and audio-visual equipment are used at conventions to convey information about careers and jobs in the truck and bus industry and you can also find out about the further education and industrial training which is an integral part of most careers connected with trucks and buses.

Be careful that you don't fall into the trap of assuming that because your parents have been happy and successful in their jobs that you can go into the same type of work and be equally successful. Everything may, of course, turn out all right in the end if you do but it is important that you have a good look at the various careers first and make your own decision on the one you wish to follow. Parental guidance and encouragement are important but this does not necessarily mean you have to walk in your father's footsteps. Avoid this temptation if you really feel you want to break away; there are many people who have already done this and been highly successful in their chosen career.

The careers officer is the first person you should contact if you are searching for a job but if you have done this and still having problems then there is no harm done in visiting your local Job Centre. There is some overlap between the Careers Service and the Job Centres as the former concentrates mainly on young people between the ages of 15 to 17 and the Job Centres deal with all age groups between 16 and 65. The Job Centres are controlled by the Employment Services Agency and provide a wide service for all types of jobs other than professional, scientific, technical and executive appointments. The Centres are usually situated in the busy part of each town and easily identifiable by their prominent Job Centre displays. Their youth advisers are trained to deal with callers in an informal and friendly manner and each Centre is part of a huge national network which makes the service particularly useful if you are seeking a job in another part of the country.

If your careers teacher, careers officer, the Job Centre, your

9

parents and friends cannot help you in your search for a job then try looking in your local newspaper and the trade magazines published mainly for readers who are in the truck and bus industry. It is also worth trying to make a direct contact with the companies you are interested in joining by making a personal visit although you may find in some cases you are told you have to make an appointment first. The Yellow Pages of the telephone directory may be useful to you if you don't know many companies in your area as they give both the telephone number and address of each firm. It has been known for some young people to secure a job simply by calling on a company and the employer being instantly impressed with the initiative of the young person that he has created a job for him on the spot. Admittedly, these occasions are few and far between but you never know your luck and if you are not appointed immediately your name and address may be filed on a waiting list to fill a vacancy that may occur in the future.

The size of a company — large or small

If you take a job with a large company part of your initial training will be concerned with the organisation of the company itself which is likely to impress you as being well-planned, comfortable to work for, with up-to-date vehicles and equipment, and ample opportunity to climb the ladder within. Most companies are generous with the opportunities they present to young people in the way of release from the company for education and training, and in-company or on-the-job training is also normally provided. People who work for large companies can usually be spared more easily for training than they can in small firms. Good working conditions with canteen or restaurant facilities, sports facilities and social activities are all normally available to people who work for large companies. There is, however, usually a great deal of competition for jobs with a large company as they spend much time and money on advertising for staff. This results in them being well-known in their area and, as they normally have a good reputation for their training facilities for young people, are often inundated with applicants for a limited number of jobs. Don't let this point deter you from applying, however, as they do take on some applicants and you may be one of the lucky ones.

There are of course disadvantages of working for a large company as well as advantages. You tend to be a small cog in a large machine and may feel insignificant and unwanted in the large team of people who are round and about you all the time. You don't always get to know much about other people's jobs as there are usually lines of demarcation between the different working groups and the different job disciplines. Movement across these lines is not encouraged by either the company or the trade unions, the latter generally being stronger in large companies than in the smaller ones. Workers in large companies often find it harder to exercise initiative in their jobs and make improvements, they find their scope is limited in what they can and cannot do. Those who wish to break the routine of their jobs find it hard to do so, and those with a flair for innovation and creative ideas find it virtually impossible to implement most of them. Large companies have a tendency to overstaff, although they are usually reluctant to admit this statement, which leads to a fair proportion of idle time in a working day leading, in turn, to frustration and loss of interest for some young people.

Working for a small company on the other hand usually presents good opportunities to learn about more, or all, aspects of the company's involvement. It doesn't take as long to get to know the people with whom you are working and, in a very small firm, it is likely that you will get to know everyone from the managing director at the top of the ladder to every single operative at the bottom of the ladder. There is a tendency to feel useful in a small company as a young person, as you may well have some small responsibility to carry in your job and if you are missing for a day, when you attend college for example, you are missed by your colleagues mainly because things are not being done in your absence. The opportunities for taking on a little more work, if you think you can cope, are better in a small company and there is more opportunity to display any initiative you may possess. You may be asked to stand in or cover for a colleague in his absence which gives an opportunity to get to know something about his job as well as your own and this all adds to a stimulation of interest in your work and career.

There are of course some disadvantages of working for a small company. You may for example find yourself having to work for long periods of time on your own which can be a lonely experience and there may be occasions when there is no one to turn to for advice and assistance if you are stuck with a job. You will find that there are more situations in a small company where it is necessary to 'make do or mend' and this leads to good training in

11

improvisation.

There are fewer facilities for social and recreation in a smaller company and prospects of advancement once you have completed your training or apprenticeship may be limited.

Job application and interview

If you have made up your mind about your career and have decided you want to work with trucks and buses then carry on reading this book as it contains a great deal of interesting and useful information.

The next step forward is to apply to one or more companies for a job. Most companies in the truck and bus industry insist that you apply by using their prescribed application form which will be issued to you on request and this can be done by calling in, writing or telephoning. It is important that you read the form carefully and study any other particulars which may be sent to you with the form before completing it with details. It is also important that you fill in the form neatly and thoroughly as it is unlikely that the person who may interview you later will know you personally and will only be able to judge your suitability for the job from the information on your form and the way in which you have presented it. If you use your best hand-writing and do not make any spelling mistakes you are more likely to make an impression on a future employer than you will if your form is written untidily and carelessly containing a number of crossings-out and a few grammatical errors. Your completed form should contain all information about you relevant to the job. If, for example, you leave out your CSE results in physics, mathematics and English and have forgotten to mention that you took a short course in traffic engineering at secondary school you will certainly reduce your chance of clinching a job in transport engineering or traffic management. If the application form is divided into sections it is necessary to complete each section as fully as possible even though you may think that some of the information for which the company is asking is irrelevant to the job. The company will no doubt have good reasons for asking for particular information and it is in your interest to supply it. When you have completed the form don't forget to sign it and include the date. The company may also require your parents to sign in addition. A specimen application form for a craft apprenticeship with a bus company is shown opposite which will give you a good idea about the information a company requires.

TRAINING DEPARTMENT

CRAFT APPRENTICESHIP APPLICATION FORM

Christian Name(s) _____   Surname _____
(Block capitals)   (Block capitals)

Date of Birth _____   Place of Birth (Town) _____

Home Address _____

tate below type of Apprenticeship in which you are interested and date free to commence:

PPRENTICESHIP _____ PLACE _____ DATE _____

urname _____   Christian Name(s) _____
Parent or Guardian)

ddress _____
different from above)

resent or last School _____   Headmaster's Name _____

ddress _____   Examinations passed
                                            or to be taken   _____

you have had previous employment, please state:

ame and Address of Employer: _____

sition held: _____   Dates: _____

ason for leaving: _____

ve you suffered from any serious ailment or disability? If so please state full details: _____
_____

do you wish to become a craft apprentice?

at are your interests and hobbies?

nature of Applicant _____   Date _____

nature of Parent or Guardian
ing approval of this application _____   Date _____

13

Your letter of application

There are some companies that do not issue a prescribed application form and it is necessary therefore to write your own letter of application for a job vacancy. This should be kept short and to the point but should contain all information relevant to the job. Write out your details on a scrap piece of paper first then copy them in your letter later. By doing it this way you can make sure your spelling and punctuation is correct and it gives you a good idea how long your letter will be. Remember that most employers claim to be busy people and they don't like to have to filter through irrelevant details searching for information pertinent to the vacancy. Keep your scrap paper with the details as you may well find it useful if you are called for an interview and asked to expand on some of the points you made in your letter. Your letter will have the same impact on an employer as a completed application form so make sure you make a good job of writing it. To assist you in writing a letter of application a specimen is given below.

23 Rolling Road
Jobton
Lancashire
1 February 1981

The Training and Personnel Officer
Highways Transport Limited
Smoky Lane
ANYTOWN, AN1 0BJ

Dear Sir

In reply to your advertisement in the *Jobton Evening News* on 27 January I would like to apply for the vacancy of apprentice heavy vehicle mechanic in your transport department.

I am 16 years of age and have recently left Moorside Comprehensive School where I obtained CSEs in the following subjects: mathematics, English language, chemistry, woodwork, metalwork and art. During my final year at school I was a prefect and represented the school in the North-west Football Championships. I am also a member of St Augustine's Youth Club.

Mr Friskey at the Careers Office explained the type of training and further education I would likely receive from your company and I would be pleased if you would consider giving me an interview so that we can discuss this matter further.

Yours faithfully

(signed) I M Hopeful

The interview

Most companies, though not all, will give an interview to an applicant. However, going for an interview can be a nerve-wracking experience and most people, whatever their age, have some feelings of fear and trepidation, regardless of whether it is the first or the twenty-first. Employers do however make an allowance for 'nerves' as the majority of them have had interviews themselves and know exactly what it is like. It is important that you prepare yourself well before the interview so that you look and feel your best in order to make a good impression. You don't need to spend an enormous sum of money on clothing to impress a prospective employer as he will be well aware that you are not a big wage earner and therefore unable to purchase expensive clothing. What he will expect though is a neat and tidy appearance, clean clothing and shoes, a tidy hair style and a clean shave or neat beard. Make sure you brush your teeth and apply a deodorant so that you will smell fresh during the interview. A tense situation during an interview can produce perspiration and a smelly applicant can be off-putting to some employers.

You need to be prepared to ask questions as well as answer them at an interview as two-way communication is regarded as being more effective for the interviewer and the interviewee. An employer will want to know a good deal about you, your outlook, your interests, and why you want to work in his company. Similarly, you will want to know something about the company for which you may shortly be working, and if you are not told what you want to know, you are expected to ask.

The truck and bus industry

The truck and bus industry is made up of a large number of companies,

15

some small, some medium sized and others that are very large. Some of these companies were started from scratch by one person and have developed and grown bigger over a period of years, others started from the beginning as larger companies, and changes in central and local government policies in past years have also had some influence on the growth and shaping of the industry. Though there are many opportunities for school leavers, and in some cases university graduates, to enter this interesting and developing industry, it is regrettable that the image of the truck and bus industry, which has been formed by some people on the outside of the industry, leaves much to be desired. In fact, most branches of engineering and transport in Britain are still regarded as 'oily rag brigades' by some people, and not sufficiently respectable to enter for a career. This sort of thinking is of course a nonsense and attitudes are changing for the better. The sooner this myth is completely dispelled the better. There will always be many other fields of interest which will continue to attract young people but to the mechanically minded, the road transport industry in all its aspects will be irresistible. The opportunities for a sound training in the truck and bus industry are comparable with those in many other industries and the prospects for rising to higher positions in engineering, traffic and management are good. There is no doubt that the industry, in the foreseeable future, will need more entrants than it has taken in the past as the number of road transport vehicles continues to increase and the industry is making every effort to publicise job opportunities and career routes so that young people, who are intending working with trucks and buses, can be informed about future prospects.

What do employers look for?

When wanting to fill a vacancy in his company, an employer will be looking for someone who will make a contribution towards improving the efficiency of his company and making it more profitable. Employers are very concerned about making sufficient profit to keep them in business, most being big thinkers with a view towards expanding their company, and most of them appreciate that one of the most important of their resources is their staff. It is therefore only natural that an employer will look after his staff and will take the greatest of care when making new appointments. When filling a vacancy therefore he will be aiming at filling the job with the young person who, in his

16

opinion, is the best available at the time he is seeking someone. He will constantly monitor the progress of the young person he appoints during the initial training period with a view towards placing him in a job situation to which he is best suited. Some employers appoint staff for a probationary period before taking them on their permanent list of employees but this should be made clear to applicants during the interview.

Choice of the right young person

It is important to both the employer and the young person applying for the job that the right choice is made during the process of selection. If a good choice is made the young person will be happy when he starts the job and the employer will be satisfied with his performance and progress but if a poor choice is made the young person will be unhappy, not very interested in the work, and continually regretting having taken on the job, while the employer will see himself as lumbered with someone who will never make the grade of a mechanic, driver, traffic clerk or whatever job for which the young person is being trained.

Selecting a young person for a job is a very difficult process for an employer and experts argue about the techniques and procedures that should be adopted in order that the best possible choice is made. However, the best you can hope for as a young person being considered for selection for a job is that your prospective employer makes the right choice and if he chooses you, then good luck.

Most young people entering the truck and bus industry can expect to embark on some form of further education and training during their early years and this is costly, even though there are training grants available to most companies. Gone for ever are the days when a young person went along to a garage for a job and the prospective employer conducted the interview of five or six minutes duration while leaning on the wing of the vehicle he was in the process of repairing. Most companies these days have a standard procedure for interviewing which takes about half an hour and more than one member of the company's staff is involved during interviewing, selecting and appointing young people. Large companies employ a training and personnel officer who has a special responsibility for arranging interviews and selection tests for applicants.

I said to you earlier 'good luck' if you have applied for a job you really wanted and have been successful. If you have applied and haven't been successful so far, keep trying, your luck will change sooner or later as job selection is a tricky business. Don't lose heart if you consider yourself to be a person who is not a 'high flyer'. Young people with high academic qualifications are not always preferred by employers to those with fewer certificates as experience has shown that some academics are not suitable for training as craftsmen or clerks. Likewise, the young 'high flyer' with a big collection of O and A levels is not likely to be very happy pursuing an apprenticeship alongside other young people who hold three or four CSEs but have a more mechanical aptitude. He is more than likely to become quickly disillusioned and frustrated with the rate of progress he is making in his career and will probably leave his employer at the earliest opportunity. There are however a few exceptions to this generalisation, for example in the situation where a young person wants to enter his father's business and will be groomed in management and business techniques alongside his practical training, or in the situation where a young person is employed on the understanding that he is being specifically trained for a management post, usually in a large company with a large labour force.

Modern trucks and buses are expected to operate over long distances at high speeds and these requirements demand high standards of reliability, safety and comfort. No one expects a vehicle to break down on the road, although this does occasionally happen! As vehicles are gradually becoming more complicated and sophisticated in design, and as road transport is continuing to play an ever-increasing role in society, it is becoming increasingly important that those people who have responsibility for vehicle maintenance and operations should be well suited to their jobs. This starts with making the right choice during the interviewing stage. The heavy vehicle mechanic or technician, for example, is not only expected to be able to maintain, service and repair vehicles, he is also expected to have the skills and ability to diagnose mechanical failures in vehicle components accurately and quickly. If this is the type of job which appeals to you, and you feel you have the interest and ability to do this work, then you should make it clear during your interview and your prospective employer will take your comments into account. Similarly, if you feel you have an interest in transportation, warehousing, storage, distribution and running operations then you may well be interested in taking up a trainee job as a routing clerk. There are many other jobs in addition to these that may be of interest to you which will be explained at a later stage in this book.

Your attitude towards the questions and the manner in which you answer them are noted by the people who conduct the interview and are taken into account together with the actual information you convey to them. Personality and personal qualities do count in your favour at an interview and most employers take a great deal of notice in the way you conduct yourself, so do bear these points in mind even though they may not be seen to be important to you. Interviews are usually conducted in a formal but kindly manner and you will be made to feel at ease during the early part of your interview so that you can give your best natural performance. You will normally be interviewed in a way which will encourage you to speak about yourself and elaborate on some of the points you made on your application form. This method makes you feel more confident and it is more effective than the type of interview which consists of a series of short abrupt questions and answers. As it is unlikely that you will have had much, if any, experience in the truck and bus industry you will not be expected to demonstrate technical or commercial knowledge about the road transport industry, although you may be expected to have read books and magazines or watched television programmes associated with road transport. You may also have gained some knowledge of travel, roadways and transport vehicles as a result of going about in your family car or by travelling by bus or coach to school or to social outings. You may also have had a little experience assisting in changing a wheel or fitting a lamp bulb on your family car. A prospective employer will listen with interest to anything you can tell him about such experiences as this is helping him to form an opinion about your suitability for the job.

Don't forget to mention your hobbies at your interview even though you may have already stated them on your application form. Whether they may be athletic or intellectual they are important. Your experience in a youth club, in the Scouts (or Guides) will also be of interest to an employer as some of these interests give him some guidance in judging the qualities of leadership you possess. This information enables him to assess your potential for future training and placement.

Selection tests

More and more employers are including tests in their selection and interviewing procedure. There is a wide variety of tests used and the type of tests you are likely to be asked to attempt depend on the kind of job for which you are applying and the qualifications already in your possession. If, for example, you have applied for a job in engineering you may well be asked to take tests in science, physics and mathematics, whereas English and geography tests may be presented to you if you have applied for a job in traffic. There is less chance of being tested in these subjects of course if you already hold CSE or GCE passes in the same subjects. Your first reaction to being asked to take tests will no doubt be 'What again—it's like being back at school', as the reasons for having to take them are not immediately obvious to most young people but, as far as employers are concerned, the tests are a good thing as they help them to fit the right person into the vacancy. It is also a fact that the days have long gone when a vehicle mechanic, driver or traffic clerk could do his job without any knowledge of English and mathematics. Virtually everyone in the truck and bus industry has to be able to fill in documents, write reports and be able to follow written instructions. Similarly, some knowledge of simple arithmetic is required: drivers have to calculate their hours of driving for their record books, mechanics have to be able to use calculations when they are measuring components for wear, and traffic clerks spend much of their time in calculating load weights and vehicle mileages. You must also bear in mind that although you may not be expected to do significant amounts of writing and calculating in the early part of your career you may well have to do a great deal in the latter part if you advance to a position in the supervisory or management grades.

Don't be too surprised if you are given a test to measure your intelligence, your spacial ability, or your mechanical reasoning, as abilities in the latter tests are regarded as vital ingredients by some companies for young people who they intend to place into apprenticeships for craftsmen and technicians. An example of a mechanical reasoning test is shown below. These tests are regarded as useful because they are very similar to the real problems that a craftsman has to solve during his career. The reasoning involved in the example given is similar to that applied by a heavy vehicle mechanic when overhauling a gear box and testing it for serviceability.

An example of a mechanical reasoning test

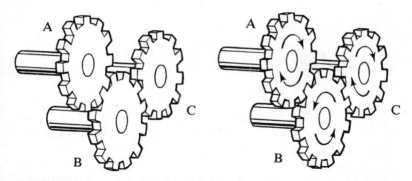

(a) Which wheel in the gear train turns round the same way as wheel A?

(b) By drawing arrows on the gears as shown it is easy to sort out. The answer is of course C.

You may also be asked to do a test so that your practical ability can be measured. There are many ways in which this type of test can be given, one being done by presenting you with a simple vehicle component already dismantled into a jumble of bits and pieces and contained in a box, and allowing you a specified period of time to sort out the jumble and assemble it correctly. You will be supplied with the necessary tools to assemble the part and it will be thoroughly checked afterwards to make sure it is correctly done.

I have explained a number of tests to you and the best advice that can accompany these explanations is—be prepared!

The industry

Trucking and busing are two of the newer transport industries and a
great deal of expansion has taken place in both of them during the
past twenty years caused mainly by the increase in the use of road
vehicles for the transportation of goods and people. The truck and
bus industry sometimes regards itself as 'third generation', this image
having emerged as a result of the many family businesses, now
firmly established, that were started as small firms by a grandfather
or other relative some thirty to forty years ago. Praiseworthy are
those early pioneers who had the initiative, foresight and enterprise
to develop transport, in some cases as a side line to their principal
field of country which could well have been coal trading, furniture
removals or ice cream vending. Some of their vehicles could be
adapted easily for different uses, one example being the flat truck
which was used for carrying goods during normal working hours
and fitted with seats and a covered frame for transporting passengers
during the evenings and weekends.

But what about the truck and bus industry of today and how does
a young person train for a career in it? The answers depend on the
size of company, the nature of its operations and the policy of
company management towards education and training. There are
also differences in the education and training policies to meet the
different requirements of the truck and bus industries.

A few statistics to start with will give you some idea of the scale of
the industry. The number of road vehicles in use in the United
Kingdom is about 17.5 million. This number is subdivided into
about 14 million cars, 1.2 million motor cycles, 1.6 million goods
vehicles and 0.11 million buses and coaches. Over a million people
are employed in the industry and road transport is the dominant
mode of transport in Britain, with lorries carrying 85% of total
goods transported. It has been reliably estimated that the road

22

transport industry will need several thousand more people in the later part of the 1980s than it employs now. There has been a significant increase in the number of women employed in the industry during the past few years and the number of craft apprentices and tradesmen has risen considerably but drivers still form the major proportion of the workforce. As these trends are likely to continue the future of the road transport industry looks promising for young people.

The truck and bus industry of today comprises many different activities and the demands on people are far more complex than in the past. Some examples of today's road transport activities which involve the use of vehicles and people are the daily deliveries of goods to shops and supermarkets necessary to replenish their shelves, the regular public services which have to be maintained by bus companies to keep their passengers satisfied, and the fuel tanker vehicles which have to deliver regular supplies of petrol and oil to garages, industrial premises, offices and houses.

Apart from the skills required for drivers of the many different types of vehicles there are other skills used in planning routes, loading and unloading goods vehicles efficiently and safely, and ensuring that passengers arrive at their destinations promptly and safely. All this means employing a highly skilled workforce based on years of experience and well accomplished in the sophisticated techniques necessary to ensure that road transport vehicles run smoothly and efficiently.

Behind the scenes of the trucks and buses that are actually operating on the roads there are large numbers of people in offices, depots and garages involved in many different jobs such as clerks, loaders, forklift truck operators, warehouse people and supervisors. Further behind the scenes are the numerous classes of engineers and maintenance staff in workshops who are responsible for making sure that their vehicles are available for service when required, and roadworthy and safe for the transportation of goods or passengers. There are other types of vehicles used for service operations which include motorway gritters, refuse collection vehicles and street sweepers.

If we take a broader look at the transport scene there are the many thousands who are employed in the manufacturing sector of the industry which includes vehicle designers, production engineers, component assemblers, computer operators and many more who are responsible for manufacturing and supplying vehicles to the operators.

There are also those employed by the Department of Transport and other government departments which deal with a wide variety of business particularly concerned with legislation and regulations appertaining to road transport. The Department of Transport is the body which controls the Heavy Goods Vehicle Testing Stations, vehicle licensing, drivers' licences and, to some extent, vehicle inspections for roadworthiness.

Trucking

Fleet transport operators

There are basically two types of operator—fleet transport operators and road hauliers. Fleet transport is a large part of the trucking industry and employs several thousand drivers and others who are responsible for a wide variety of operations within the public and private sectors of the industry. It is convenient to consider public transport at three levels; national, regional or area, and local. At national level, government departments and public corporations operate hundreds of trucks and vans for many different purposes. Department of Transport gritters are used to keep the motorways clear in the winter months, telephone cable laying and repairs require a reliable transport service operated by the Post Office, and outside television broadcasts give a need for a wide variety of vehicles operated by the BBC. You can no doubt think of many other examples besides these.

You will also have noticed trucks and vans which are operated by regional or area authorities. The Electricity Boards have fleets of vehicles ranging from small vans used by service engineers to make visits to premises to repair cookers, washing machines, refrigerators and other electrical appliances, to heavy trucks used for transporting large electrical units for industrial purposes. Similarly the Gas Boards and Water Authorities have large fleets of vehicles for a variety of work, some of the latter's being adapted to draw trailers carrying emergency water supplies or pumps. The Area Health Authorities also operate different types of vehicles, two examples being the Blood Transfusion Service personnel carriers and the Mobile Chest X-ray service vehicles operated by regional health authorities. The police authorities, in addition to the hundreds of motor cycles and patrol cars, have a range of larger trucks and coaches which include horse carriers and personnel buses. Another spectacular class of vehicles operated by area authorities are fire engines. The fire brigades have some interesting vehicles and it is well worth paying a visit to a fire station to see some of them.

Public transport at the local level is so frequently seen that it tends to be taken for granted. Street lighting vehicles are in service for twenty-four hours a day for transporting lighting engineers and equipment from the local authority's engineering workshops to the lamps on the roadways. Local education authority school meals vans are in regular use delivering meals to schools, and we all expect these vehicles to be reliable and deliver on time. On the rare occasion when a school dinner arrives late as a result of a truck breakdown it doesn't take long before the driver, the truck, or the local authority are given the blame—particularly if the meal is cold as well as late! This point emphasises the need for a reliable vehicle maintenance service and a responsible workforce if breakdowns are to be kept to a minimum. Vehicles are also used by other departments of local authorities for the maintenance of highways, street cleansing, library services and the care of parks and recreation areas.

In addition to the public transport sector fleet operators are the private and independent users of vehicles. These include bakeries, breweries, and supermarket companies. The transportation of food, drink, refrigerated goods and clothing is carried out with the use of many different types of trucks, some small, some large, some with open flat platform bodies and some with containers. It is worth looking at the delivery bays of your local supermarket if you are interested in seeing some of these trucks.

In addition to the fleet transport operators mentioned are H M Services: the Army, the Navy and the Air Force. Several thousand vehicles are operated by these Services which include some interesting special purpose vehicles. You would normally have to join one of the Services to work on these vehicles although they employ a small number of civilians.

Road hauliers

The road haulage sector of the industry is that part which operates its vehicles for 'hire and reward' which means that it carries goods for people and charges them for the service it provides. You may have noticed Haulage Contractor or Road Haulage marked on the cab door of some goods vehicles together with the company's name, address and telephone number which helps them to advertise that they are in the haulage business. Some road hauliers are one-man businesses where the owner is driver, loader and unloader, clerk and 'jack of all trades'. At the other end of the scale there are hauliers with several thousands of vehicles in their fleets. Some hauliers concentrate on operating locally and seldom travel outside a 30 to 40 mile radius from their base centre while at the other extreme, others operate internationally and may be away from base for several weeks at a time.

There are some hauliers who operate a flexible free and easy policy of carrying goods anywhere at any time of the day or night for their customers. Others operate a trunk service which may involve three drivers to each truck. An example of a trunk service is where a day driver picks up a load during the daytime and drives back to Depot 1 by evening. A night truck driver then takes over the truck and drives from Depot 1 to Depot 2 a distance of say 300 miles travelling overnight and arriving in the early hours of the morning. A third driver is waiting at Depot 2 to take over the lorry, drive it to its ultimate destination during the early part of the day, and deliver the goods. He then drives on to another pick-up point to take on another load and heads for Depot 2 where he arrives in the evening. The night trunk driver is waiting at Depot 2 to take over the truck after having his sleep and rest during the day and drives overnight back to Depot 1 arriving in the early morning. There the day driver takes over and shunts the vehicle to its destination for unloading. He then moves on to another pick-up point to re-load the vehicle and the trunk cycle re-commences.

The road haulage industry consists of a mixture of private and public businesses and state-owned companies. Some of the businesses were started several decades ago by individuals or families and are still surviving today. Other companies started privately or publicly and were nationalised in the late 1940s becoming part of British Road Services. Some of the owners and staff went in with BRS taking jobs with the state-owned company while some of the other owners sold their trucks and premises and left the haulage business. As a result of these changes quite a number of the old established haulage businesses were never to be seen or heard of again.

British Road Services

British Road Services continued to grow bigger and bigger during the late 1940s and early '50s as it continued to absorb more and more private and public companies. However, the middle '50s witnessed further changes in nationalised transport due to a change in government, and its new policies on transport gave an opportunity for some of the old companies to start up in business again as independents and in competition with BRS. From that period onwards there has been healthy competition between independent hauliers and BRS together with National Carriers, Roadline and others, which all compete in a free market for business.

The road haulage scene today consists of many different shapes and sizes of trucks. Some hauliers operate trucks with flat platform bodies with the load covered by tarpaulin sheets, others use box van bodies or enclosed bodies using flexible curtain sides. The latter two types have the advantage of better load protection, physical load security, and less risk of pilfering. Other hauliers specialise in operating low-loader vehicles to transport heavy bulky loads, some weighing over 100 tonnes, many being classified as 'abnormal and indivisible' loads. Giant electrical transformers, ship components and aircraft sections are some examples of loads carried on heavy low-loaders. You may have already seen some of these heavy outfits, sometimes known as road trains, travelling slowly along the road-way and comprising of two towing tractor units at the front and a cab on the rear of the trailer. Other combinations may use a towing tractor and a pushing tractor at the rear together with a third driver in the trailer cab whose job it is to steer the trailer which is necessary when negotiating tight corners. These outfits are usually accompanied by a police escort which adds to the spectacular and exciting nature of such a scene.

Other hauliers specialise in tanker transport for the carriage of milk, petrol, oil, sulphuric acid and many other liquids which are transported in bulk. The drivers of tankers have a very responsible job and are specially trained to cope with breakdowns, accidents and hazards which may present danger, as some tankers are capable of carrying as much as 27 276 litres (6000 gallons).

Tipping lorries are another specialisation in road haulage. These

27

Road hauliers

are used for a variety of operations which include the delivery of materials to building sites and the carriage of waste materials from industrial premises.

Company structure

The structure of a road haulage company and the transport division of a company operating its own fleet of vehicles is usually based on the pattern shown in the chart below with the functions and staff divided into two main groups of traffic and engineering. The former group, sometimes known as the transport department, functions by allocating vehicles to loads, and loads to vehicles, and monitoring vehicle movement. It is sometimes referred to as the nerve centre of a haulage company as the company's existence and future depends to a large extent on the effectiveness and efficiency of this department. There are periods during a working day when this department is extremely busy and bustling with activity and there are other periods when it is comparatively quiet. When bustling with activity, the vehicles are being turned out to a new job and destination or are returning to base after completing a journey. During these periods the transport staff are issuing drivers with information and instructions on their new jobs and collecting delivery documents from drivers

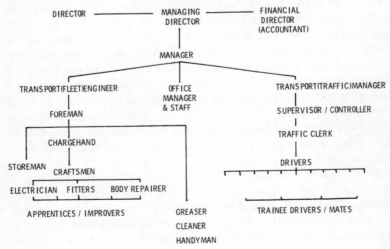

who have completed their jobs and returned to base for further instructions. During their quiet spells the transport staff are kept busy planning for future trafficking.

The company's engineering department is usually headed by a transport (fleet) engineer who is also very active. The engineer is responsible for making sure that the company's vehicles are well maintained and available as much as is possible for the transport department to use. Regular maintenance, servicing and inspections of vehicles are carried out by the engineering department on a planned basis whereby each vehicle is regularly maintained according to a mileage or time based programme. By using a planned preventative maintenance programme the vehicles are kept in good mechanical condition and breakdowns are kept to a minimum which makes the vehicles available for use by the transport department for most of the time. This is an important point in the world of trucks and buses as company managers like to see vehicles being available for trafficking as much as possible. The company can only make a profit when its trucks are on the road and carrying goods for customers. When a vehicle is broken down on the roadside or in the workshop it is losing money for the company, so it is important that 'downtime' is kept to a minimum.

Apprenticeships

As most young people start their careers as apprentices or trainees it is better to start at the bottom of the chart (page 28) and gradually move upwards. Apprenticeships have been part of industry for many years as a means of providing industrial training for young people entering employment and they are still extensively used in the truck and bus industry as the main system of passing on craft skills and techniques. The apprenticeship is a form of employment that involves both employer and employee, the former agreeing to take on a young person and train him in the fundamental skills of his occupation whilst the latter agrees to learn and benefit from the training and accepts a relatively low wage during the period of apprenticeship. The apprenticeship system has a number of advantages and disadvantages to both the employer and the apprentice. On the one hand it tends to be rigid and binding for both parties and its lack of flexibility sometimes leads to difficulties in cases where it becomes desirable to cancel the apprenticeship. On the other hand, the system provides for continuity and security for the young person which are necessary if he is going to benefit from the long and sometimes tedious period of training.

Following a trial period Deeds of Indenture may be signed by the apprentice, his parent or guardian, and his employer, which make the apprenticeship a legal contract binding all three parties. The actual type of Deed used varies depending upon company policy and may be written out on a National Joint Council document, or it may be a private agreement. The Deed usually states the type of training that will be given to the apprentice, the period during which the training will be given, the arrangements for release from work to attend college for further education and training, the wages to be paid, and several other conditions of employment. In return, the apprentice agrees to stay with the company for the agreed period and do his best to fulfil his part of the agreement. Deeds tend to work in favour of the apprentice and give less protection to the employer.

The duration of apprenticeships in the truck and bus industry are usually between four and five years the actual length depending upon the young person's age on starting with the company, his background, his ability, and the training policy of his company. Most employers today regard their employees as their most important resource and feel that they should give as good a training as possible to their young people. Although all training is costly for the company they consider it as money well spent, as a highly qualified and trained staff is important for their future survival.

Some companies carry out all training on their own premises and release apprentices to attend college for further education by the day release system. Others release their young people for some of their industrial training as well as further education. Whichever of these systems is used depends on company policy. You can however rest assured that the days have long gone when an employer looked upon his apprentice as a form of cheap labour to brew the tea and run errands for the chips and pies at lunchtime. The vast majority of companies take training seriously these days and accept that there are few immediate returns from apprentices as training is considered to be more of a long-term investment.

A wide variety of work is carried out in most engineering departments of transport companies and this requires many different skills, expertise, ability and knowledge. The ratio of apprentices to skilled staff also varies considerably between companies but a fairly typical road haulage company would employ one apprentice to every three craftsmen. The largest proportion of apprentices are usually mechanics but there may also be an auto-electrician, a body repairer and possibly an apprentice partsman in the company. One of the most important requirements for good quality maintenance and repairs of trucks and buses is an organised and formalised system of training and education for all apprentices in a company. Although some of today's transport engineers started their careers as apprentices learning by the traditional system of 'sitting next to Nellie' they would be amongst the first to admit that this system is not suitable for young people of today. The skills and responsibilities of a skilled craftsman today are far more complex and sophisticated than ever before and although they find their work very rewarding and worthwhile their training needs to be planned right from the beginning.

Evidence of having served an apprenticeship is important and documents containing such evidence should therefore be obtained from an employer when training is completed. Young people should carefully preserve these documents as they may be required when seeking promotion or wishing at a later stage to change employer. The RTITB document system is invaluable to apprentices and employers as a record of the training objectives and standards achieved during training. Documentary evidence other than Deeds of Apprenticeship can be obtained from some employers in the form of a Certificate of Completion of Training which the employer presents to the young person after his training is completed. This is a simpler and less binding form of certification than the Indenture and some employers favour this idea. Registration with a National Joint Council or with an appropriate trade union is also a means of obtaining written documents to vouch for having served an apprenticeship.

Some companies divide the apprenticeship period into two parts with the first two years consisting of training for junior apprentices and the latter two or three years consisting of more advanced training for senior apprentices or improvers. A young person progressively becomes more skilled at his work as his apprenticeship continues for which he receives a progressive annual increase in his rate of pay up to the age of 20 or 21 when he completes his training and becomes entitled to the full rate of pay as a craftsman.

The specialists jobs

A transport department normally employs a far greater number of heavy vehicle mechanics (fitters) than other specialist craftsmen and the proportion of apprentices tends to be in the same ratio as craftsmen. As apprentice mechanics usually outnumber apprentice auto-electricians, partsmen and body repairers it is best to look at the job and responsibilities of the skilled mechanic first.

The heavy vehicle mechanic (fitter)

A heavy vehicle mechanic has to deal with a wide range of work which may include routine servicing, maintaining, repairing and inspecting trucks and buses to keep them roadworthy and safe. He is a skilled craftsman trained to high standards to cope with the complexities of modern goods and passenger vehicles, and his job carries a good deal of responsibility with it. He may also be responsible for diagnosing faults on a vehicle before he actually does the job and may also be the vehicle tester who checks the completed job to make sure that the vehicle is in a fit condition to go back onto the road after repair.

Job satisfaction

Most people already employed in the truck and bus industry would be ready to admit, if asked, that they find their job interesting and rewarding. No two days are exactly the same for a heavy vehicle mechanic as his work is so varied. A mechanic may well find himself tackling an engine repair one day and adjusting a vehicle's brakes the next day. Some jobs may take as little as half-an-hour to complete while others may take several days. One of the most satisfying periods for a mechanic is when he has completed a repair job on a vehicle and he sees it going back into service.

Reliable workmanship is very important in the heavy vehicle repair industry as trucks and buses are expected to perform reliably in service. A broken down vehicle presents problems for the driver and the company management and if a vehicle has failed as a result of bad workmanship on the part of the mechanic he is not going to be very popular. For example, no transport manager is going to be very pleased with a mechanic who has not done a complete service on a container truck when instructed to and as a result the vehicle has broken down on the motorway loaded with 20 tonnes of fish. There will not only be the unpleasant smell of rotting fish to tolerate but also the risk of losing a valuable customer who has been let down on a delivery date and time. A high standard of workmanship is absolutely essential.

Training to be a heavy vehicle mechanic is very different from training to be a light vehicle (car) mechanic. For example, heavy mechanics must have a sound knowledge of diesel engines and understand how compressed air braking systems operate. As most components on a heavy vehicle are heavier than car components there is a great deal to learn about handling components and using workshop equipment to make the job easier and safer.

The auto-electrician

In the early days of road transport it was not uncommon to see mechanics tackling electrical repairs on trucks and buses in addition to the mechanical jobs but this is a sight rarely to be seen today. Garages where these exceptions are most likely to be found are in the small companies which operate a few vehicles and employ only one or two craftsmen who have developed a fair amount of craft versatility and are sometimes known as 'all-rounders'. It is far more common to see electrical work being done in garages by skilled auto-electricians who have served a different style of apprenticeship than the mechanics and because of their different training are specialists in their own right. The auto-electrician, sometimes nicknamed 'sparks', is also trained differently from the domestic and industrial electrician. He has little contact with 'mains' supplies of electricity. His vehicles operate with 24 volt or 12 volt electrical circuits which are quite different from 'mains' circuits and demand different skills and experience to maintain and repair.

The auto-electrician is specifically trained as a craftsman or technician and his training programme is arranged to suit the needs of his company. The first year of his training may follow the same training pattern as a mechanic as it is often considered to be a good thing if a first-year apprentice electrician learns something about the basic principles of the engineering aspects of trucks and buses alongside his fellow mechanics. But once the first year of training is completed the two classes of apprentices go their own separate ways and finally qualify as distinctly separate tradesmen.

The ability to use ammeters and voltmeters is a 'must' for the auto-electrician as he requires these instruments to diagnose electrical faults in circuits and components. He must also possess the basic craft skills required for soldering and brazing as these are sometimes necessary to enable him to join cables together or to fix connecting terminals to cables. He also needs to know about the behaviour of vehicle batteries and be able to test them for condition. An example of an electrician's job on a vehicle would be a breakdown caused by a discharged (flat) battery. He would be expected to investigate the cause of the discharged battery and rectify the fault which he found to be the source of the cause. This may involve a systematic checking of a number of electrical components before the trouble spot is diagnosed. It may then be necessary to make an adjustment, carry out a repair, or replace the defective component to put the job right.

An auto-electrician also needs to have a knowledge of vehicle lighting regulations. Extra lamps, for example, have to be fitted according to regulations and light beams need checking regularly to make sure that they are aligned properly so as not to dazzle other road users or lose their effectiveness for seeing purposes. Another example of some of the problems that an auto-electrician has to sort out is the 'crackling' interference on the radio of a coach or truck. To do this type of work requires a knowledge of radio and aerial fitting, together with some know-how on fitting radio suppressors.

An auto-electrician is a key man in a garage and has an important part to play in the smooth running of a fleet of vehicles. If you feel that you have an aptitude for electrical work then it is well worth considering a career in the field of auto-electrics as it can prove to be very interesting to the right person.

The body repair specialist

Vehicle body repairers, more commonly known as 'panel beaters' in the transport industry, use a wide variety of skills in their work. The range of work actually covered largely depends upon the size of the company and its policy regarding their direct involvement in body repairs.

In some garages the body repairer may be mainly employed to

deal with accident damage on vehicles which involves the knocking-out of dents and bumps in wings, cabs and body panels. Where new panels are to be fitted to a vehicle the body repairer may have to rely on his 'hand skills' to shape body components so that they will fit the vehicle properly, whilst a repairer in another body shop may be able to take advantage of specialised equipment and machines for the folding and bending of steel components which places less reliance on 'hand skills'.

A body repairer also needs to know how to join panels together and fix them securely to the vehicle body. This type of work involves other skills in the use of fasteners, rivet guns, or in the techniques necessary to weld or braze components. A great deal of training is necessary in order to handle welding and brazing equipment safely and properly which includes safety training and precautions, use of the correct gas pressures and flame adjustments, and a knowledge of metals. Some garages are equipped with both gas and electric welding plants.

The upholstery in truck cabs and bus saloons may also be the responsibility of the body repairer and he may be expected to be able to carry out repairs on upholstery whilst having to ensure that its appearance is not impaired. Other skills are required to handle a vehicle's trim, and a knowledge of rust treatment, necessary to combat corrosion, is expected from a body repairer.

More and more new vehicles are being built with glass reinforced plastic components and a repairer needs to know how to handle these materials which are vastly different from metals. There are several advantages in using glass reinforced plastics for truck cabs and other components but one of the advantages, as far as body repairers are concerned, is its inflexibility. A slight knock on the corner of a cab may well result in a large chunk of material falling off, whereas a steel cab would only suffer a dent which could easily be knocked out by a repairer. There are also health and safety hazards to be aware of when working on plastics.

Another range of skills used by a body repairer is in the use of body straightening equipment such as pushers, pull dozers, hydraulic pressing jacks, and jigs for aligning bodies, all of these being particularly useful for use on vehicles which have been involved in road accidents and collisions.

The parts person

The partsman, better known in most garages as the storeman or storekeeper, is another interesting job worth considering for a boy or girl about to leave school and considering a career in the transport industry. The partsman's main aim is to carry out his work as efficiently as possible by making sure that parts are available for supplying to mechanics and other craftsmen when required. A partsman must be able to identify parts quickly and be familiar with the technical terms used in garages, bearing in mind that a component may have two or even three different names. His expertise is acquired by years of training and experience and a good partsman (or partswoman) is just as important an asset to a company as a good mechanic or auto-electrician.

His initial training covers the same basic studies as a mechanic and an auto-electrician so that he can make himself familiar with the terms used in the workshop and be able to recognise components as they appear on the vehicles. His further training includes the more specialised aspects of stores control which includes the ability to understand fully manufacturers' parts lists, manuals and spares catalogues. He is trained to make the best use of his location and storage facilities. This means he has to know which of the stock items are the fast-moving ones and which are the slow ones. Fast moving spares have to be easily and quickly accessible and are therefore stored close to the serving hatch or the doorway so that they can be issued quickly to the craftsmen. If the stores area is not well organised there will be much time wasted by mechanics in waiting for spares at the stores and unnecessary 'downtime' for the vehicles. Company directors never feel very happy when they see mechanics leaning on the serving hatch lighting-up a cigarette while waiting several minutes to be served with the parts they require for an urgent repair on a vehicle. On the other hand, directors are happy when they see a quick and efficient service being performed by the partsman which is only possible if he is properly trained. There is also the clerical function of the partsman which consists of ordering parts, stock-taking, spot-checking and handling documentation. Some knowledge of arithmetic and clear handwriting are required for this work if it is to be carried out accurately. In addition to the control of parts some partsmen have responsibility for storing special tools and equipment for use by the craftsmen in the garage.

Another function of partsmen in some companies is to deal with customers who visit from outside the company. This service requires tact and diplomacy as outside customers expect to be treated with courtesy when buying parts and if they do not receive the treatment they expect they may well do their shopping at another company where they are politely received. The loss of customers is something else that company directors become displeased about which makes training in customer relations essential for a progressive company.

The truck and bus salesperson

Although the majority of truck and bus salespeople are mature and experienced, some opportunities to train for this interesting career do however exist. As the selling of vehicles is of immense importance to manufacturers and distributors, the need to recruit young people with suitable personal qualities for this career is also important. A salesperson needs knowledge and skill to do his job well and his training usually consists of planned in-company training with additional training obtained by attending courses at the manufacturers' training schools and the RTITB Motecs.

One of the first things a trainee salesperson has to learn is how to sell himself. This comes before selling anything else as far as a customer is concerned, and it means that he needs to be particular about his appearance and the way he approaches and speaks to people. He needs to be smartly dressed, this does not necessarily mean in expensive clothing, well groomed, have a neat and tidy hair style, and clean shoes. He has to be a good listener as well as a good talker, and the development of a good telephone technique is also important. When in conversation with customers he is expected to show enthusiasm for the goods he is selling and this means maintaining a pleasant and friendly manner showing patience with his customers at all times and being careful not to express any personal prejudices on topics such as religion and race.

A salesperson needs to be able to test drive and demonstrate the vehicles he is trying to sell and this usually means that a HGV driving licence is required. Technical knowledge is also important as a salesperson has to be able to advise on the most suitable vehicle for the customer's needs and this requires a sound knowledge of such technical items as gearbox ratios, braking system types and retarders, engine data on brakepower, torque and fuel consumption, and so on. Vehicle specifications, such as the number of axles, the gross weight of goods vehicles, the seating capacity of passenger vehicles, the types of body available, the need for a tail-lift on a truck, or two or more doorways on a bus, all require discussing with customers and sound advice is expected from salespeople on all these matters as a great deal of money is spent in the purchase of heavy vehicles.

Another dimension of knowledge is required in the field of legislation and licensing, and some knowledge of finance is also needed. The salesperson selling a new vehicle has to be able to make a value judgement on a used vehicle that a customer may wish to trade in as a part exchange for a new one which demands a good up-to-date understanding of the current market situation.

Dealing with customers involves an ability on the part of the salesperson to negotiate at various levels with companies with which he is selling and a decision made by a buyer may make a deal of several thousand pounds, or in the case of large fleet operators, hundreds of thousands of pounds. Selling trucks and buses can be really big business.

Salespeople are not only expected to negotiate with established customers but also are expected to make new contacts with a view towards increasing their company's sales and this means they are expected to get around to hauliers, operators and bus companies and make face-to-face contact with new customers and find out what their future requirements are so that they can do their best to satisfy their needs. This type of personal contact builds up confidence in customers and invariably leads to more success in dealing and selling to customers than does the more impersonal, though admittedly quicker, approach by telephone.

Career progression is possible from salesperson to sales manager or sales executive and added responsibilities are taken on with the higher status and salary. A manager may be responsible for co-ordinating sales within the department he controls and he is responsible for fostering and maintaining high standards of business ethics and public relations as the company's image is, to a large extent, reflected by its sales staff. The manager is also responsible for long-range selling and marketing objectives as well as having experience to prepare quotations and deal with the finances of his department. Appointments at manager and executive level are usually filled by salespeople who have a proven record of successful selling.

You will already no doubt appreciate that a wide range of experience, knowledge, personal effort and determination is needed to become a successful salesperson. His job can be both interesting and rewarding as it often involves dealing with many different people at a variety of levels in a number of different companies. Financial rewards vary but usually consist of a basic salary plus a commission or bonus and use of a company car.

The engineering foreman/woman

Most foremen are appointed from the ranks of craftsmen, usually mechanics, and advance via the intermediate stages of senior or leading craftsman and chargehand (see page 28). A foreman's job is usually regarded as the first stage in the higher careers of management and is one of the hardest jobs to do properly and effectively, and often found to be demanding mentally and physically. This doesn't mean that the job is not worth considering as a career, on the contrary, it can be a challenging and rewarding job with plenty of scope and interest, and it can be the start of a suitable training for some of the higher positions in management. As a foreman is employed in 'first-line' management he is usually regarded as the 'boss' by the apprentices as he represents the company's authority.

The foreman is both a technical person and an administrator and may be either a working foreman on the shop floor or an administrative foreman mainly involved in handling documents and attending to 'paper work' depending on the type of company in which he is employed. As most foremen have risen from the ranks of craftsmen they have an understanding of some of the problems with which craftsmen have to cope, and they are usually the people to whom craftsmen turn when advice is required or assistance is needed on a job. The foreman's technical knowledge and experience is often needed to solve a problem on the shop floor and he is usually well respected for his competence in dealing with problems which frequently occur.

In addition to being a master craftsman, the foreman is expected to have an understanding of human relations as he is the 'middle man' or 'buffer' between the craftsmen and other workers on the shop floor and higher management. He has to be able to deal with, and handle, people at all levels, and to do this type of work means that he must also be a good communicator. He is expected to keep the people below himself informed about new developments and changes in company policy as he receives these from higher management and he is also expected to keep management informed about what's going on on the shop floor.

The foreman must possess the personal qualities required to be a good 'leader' of the staff he controls and to make himself accessible for advice and consultation with the craftsmen and other people for whom he is responsible.

The way that he treats people under his control is important if good working relationships are to be fostered and maintained. He has to be fair in the way that he treats his staff and not show any favouritism or prejudice as these lead to bad feeling amongst workers and their morale is lowered. A foreman is better respected if he is helpful and constructive in his attitude and makes time to listen sympathetically to the complaints and suggestions of workers.

Some foremen are known as working foremen which implies that they spend most of their time in the working area on the shop floor, whilst others function more as administrators and are office bound for most of the time. Whichever type of function they carry out, and this depends on company policy, their main task is to motivate their staff so that the quality of work and the throughput of jobs are as high as it is possible to achieve. Other duties which form part of a foreman's job include the responsibility and authority for inspecting and road testing vehicles, advising drivers away from base by telephone about procedures for dealing with breakdowns, and dealing with training schemes for apprentices.

The chargehand

Some companies employ a chargehand whose job is mainly to assist the foreman in his duties and lend a hand to the craftsmen when required. The chargehand has normally been promoted from a craftsman and rises to a foreman's position after gaining some experience in his job. He is the person who deputises for the foreman in his absence and is available at other times for advice and assistance to craftsmen and apprentices as well as having some regular work to do in the garage, workshop or foreman's office.

The transport (fleet) engineer

The transport engineer has management status in his company and has a wide span of responsibilities for the people he controls and the vehicles for which he is responsible. His particular role depends upon the size of his company and its policy but he invariably is a management person and spends little of his time actually repairing vehicles, although he carries the responsibility for ensuring that work in the engineering department is carried out properly and efficiently. His position in the company carries authority and it is surprising how quickly some of the young people in an engineering department start to admire the status and work performed by their transport engineer and set their sights ultimately to becoming an engineer.

The fleet engineer needs the skills and experience to be able to make mature value judgements on all matters that affect the staff and vehicles under his control. He also has to be able to answer to the people senior to himself for the work being done in his department. His day-to-day work involves having to make decisions that affect staff and vehicle availability and he is frequently involved with issues which include labour relations, wage negotiations and working conditions where liaison with trade union representatives sometimes becomes necessary.

As a manager he takes a share in his company's policy decisions which, for example, may mean having a say about some of the design features of vehicles the company is about to buy which include the type and size of engine, the style of body, and the type of suspension. His experience includes special knowledge and skills which are suited to the types of vehicles operated by his company, such as flat platform trucks, tippers, tankers, and low-loaders. He may also have some control of the spending of his company's money on vehicles, parts and workshop equipment which makes it necessary for him to be able to cost and quantify the work within his department.

He is responsible for a large number of documents and records connected with vehicle maintenance which have to be filed and kept for future reference by the company and they may be required for checking by the officers of the Department of Transport for a variety of different reasons.

He has to make sure that his orders to the foreman are properly

41

DIAMOND HAZARD WARNING SIGNS

INFLAMMABLE LIQUIDS

Black symbol on
red background

INFLAMMABLE SOLIDS

Black symbol on white background
with vertical red stripes

TOXIC GASES

Black symbol
on white background

OTHER COMPRESSED GASES

Black symbol on
green background

CORROSIVE SUBSTANCES

Black symbol on white(upper half)
and black(lower half) background

SPONTANEOUSLY COMBUSTIBLE SUBSTANCES

Black symbol on white(upper half)
and red(lower half) background

Warning signs

(a) Transport engineers who are responsible for vehicles that carry hazardous substances need to understand matters relating to the displaying of warning signs onto vehicles (left)

(b) There are regulations relating to the fitting of these rear marks which need to be understood by transport engineers (above)

carried out so that a high standard of work in the garage and workshops is maintained, this being necessary to ensure that 'downtime' is kept to a minimum and the vehicles are available for use by the traffic department as much as possible.

Goods vehicle operators have to comply with government legislation if they want to apply for, and keep, their operators' licence, and this implies that qualified staff have to be employed by companies to maintain vehicles and take responsibility for the standard of maintenance. Vehicle inspections for roadworthiness and pre-Department of Transport testing is the responsibility of the transport engineer together with a knowledge of road transport law. He must know, for example, what type of Long Vehicle markers to fit and which type of diamond hazard warning sign to display on the vehicles under his control. (See facing page and above)

The transport engineer has to have the ability to motivate all the staff in his department and have the personal qualities of initiative, drive, tact, determination and imagination to obtain the results from his staff that are conducive to efficient running of his department and the approval of his superiors. Staff appointments, training and liaison with vehicle and component manufacturers are some of the other functions of an engineer, and a large company with several branches may employ a number of assistant engineers who report to a chief engineer at the head office.

Promotion for the fleet engineer is possible in some companies and he can progress to a company manager or managing director on the company's board.

Today's drivers

The right-hand side of the chart (page 28) shows the people who are more closely connected with the trafficking side of the road haulage company and a large number of the people who work in the traffic department are drivers. Driving a truck is a professional job today and can be very rewarding and interesting although it carries a great deal of responsibility. The system for the training is not as formalised as those laid down for the training of craftsmen although there is a new scheme which enables young people to be trained for a heavy goods vehicle driving licence and this is explained in another part of this book.

Some of today's drivers started their careers at the age of 16 by taking up employment as driver's mates, sometimes known as second mates, who assisted the driver to load and unload the truck. Others started by working in goods yards where they gained experience in loading and unloading together with sheeting and roping loads on trucks. After reaching the age of 17 they took a driving test for a car licence which qualifies them to drive a light goods vehicle up to 3.5 tonnes weight. They then had a long wait up to the age of 21 when they became eligible to take a HGV test to drive a heavy goods vehicle.

If you are considering taking up driving as a career you must think carefully about working irregular and unsocial hours as this is an integral part of many driving jobs although there are, of course, some exceptions. Driving as a career can also be a lonely job as many hours may be spent behind the driving wheel travelling up and down the Motorways without anyone else to talk to. Some of today's trucks are fitted with radios which may be used by drivers to relieve monotony on long distance journeys but most drivers consider their radios as aids for partly solving the problems of loneliness and look forward to regular breaks at Motorway Services and transport cafés where they can pull-in for a sandwich and drink and chat to their colleagues.

A knowledge of geography is essential for all drivers whether they are on short distance or long distance journeys. The ability to read maps and follow instructions from a routing clerk are necessary particularly when operating vehicles through European and other overseas countries. There is an increase in international trafficking for some hauliers and their drivers may be away from head office and home for several days or even weeks in foreign countries and have to rely almost entirely on their prescribed route and maps.

Driving may be a clean job, as is fairly common with trunk driving, or it may be a dirty or dangerous job where protective clothing must be worn. Drivers who are responsible for handling loads need to be trained in the correct methods of handling goods for their own safety as well as the safety and avoidance of damage to the goods. Some companies supply their drivers with overalls which have the company name on the back, or their logo on the front pocket, which adds towards promoting the image of the company to the public. Special training is given to drivers of vehicles that carry dangerous cargos which includes the procedures to be adopted if the vehicle breaks down or has to be 'parked-up' overnight. Drivers engaged on long-distance operations need to understand and obey the law and the regulations which apply to drivers' hours and rest periods, and comply with the many regulations governing the safe handling of their vehicles, such as knowing it is an offence to leave a vehicle unattended without stopping the engine and securely applying the handbrake.

Maximum speed limits on restricted roads and motorways must be observed by drivers, fog codes must be adhered to when driving in foggy conditions, and marker boards for overhanging and projecting loads need to be displayed when carrying certain types of loads. An understanding of the powers of the police is necessary for every driver. For example, a uniformed police officer has the authority to signal a driver to stop and he has no option but to obey. Drivers must also know how to arrange for police escorts when driving long vehicles with indivisible loads through narrow roads in towns or villages. The Road Traffic Act 1972 makes it an offence to drive or attempt to drive or be in charge of a vehicle when 'having consumed alcohol in such a quantity that the proportion in the blood exceeds the prescribed limit of 80 milligrammes of alcohol per 100 millilitres of blood. A police constable in uniform can require a driver to take a breath test at the roadside if:

(a) he has reasonable cause to suspect that the driver has alcohol in his body,

(b) he has reasonable cause to suspect the driver of having committed a moving traffic offence,

(c) the driver has been involved in an accident.

As the driver depends on his licence for his livlihood it would be foolish for him to consume alcoholic drinks which exceeded the prescribed limit thereby putting him at risk of losing his licence and perhaps his job as well.

Some of the more practical skills required from drivers are the ability to manoeuvre vehicles in confined spaces and to be able to reverse semi-trailers or nose draw-bar trailers into bays for loading and unloading. When on the road a driver is expected to be able to use his brakes and gears intelligently as this is essential for road safety reasons as well as for preserving the condition of the vehicle. A good driver develops a sixth sense for changing gear at the right time and this requires him to be a good judge of his road speed and engine speed if he is to make a silent gearchange quickly and smoothly.

The transport (traffic) manager

This is another interesting job in the world of road transport and one which is worth considering as a future career. It is not, however, I hasten to add, a 'cushy number', far from it, in fact, it is one of the most demanding jobs in transport and carries a heavy responsibility with it. It is a job which often demands long and irregular hours of duty, a job which requires the ability to work, at times, under pressure, a job which needs a sense of humour to get over those hard days where there has been some aggro to cope with, and yet it is a professional job which carries a good deal of job satisfaction with it.

The manager's knowledge of transport law and regulations must be adequate enough to be able to cope with the matters relating to the law and the regulations which apply to his company's vehicles and the type of operations carried out. He is expected to maintain a good working relationship with the drivers and, at the same time, be responsible and accountable to higher management for his actions and decisions. He has to be able to communicate with the people for whom the company is carrying, and look after the business in hand, as well as keeping an eye on potential customers for whom there may be a chance of carrying in the future. He needs to be articulate enough to be able to liaise with the police, the Department of Transport, the employers' associations, the trade unions, and other bodies in the transport world.

His day-to-day responsibilities, some of which may be delegated to a traffic clerk and secretary, include the smooth running of the transport side of the business, negotiating with current and new customers to maintain and increase if possible the company's share of the carrying market in which they specialise, and dealing with the documentation which flows in a number of different directions with himself sitting at the hub of virtually everything that is going on.

Some transport managers have progressed to their present jobs as a result of having served many years in transport and most of them have a vast knowledge of the transport scene knowing it inside out. Some managers started their careers as drivers and progressed in their company through foreman driver and traffic clerk to their present position. Others started off as trainee managers by taking a junior trainee's job in the traffic office and gained their experience and qualifications which ultimately led them to their managers position in the company.

There is a great deal to learn about operating a fleet of vehicles and a manager's aim is to keep his vehicles on the road as much as possible—stationary trucks don't earn anything for the company. Managers must have good knowledge of the geography of the area in which their trucks operate and they should have the skill to be able to find out information on areas where their trucks do not normally operate. A specialised knowledge of shipping, docks, warehouses, loading bays, containerisation, tipping sites, parking compounds and overnight accommodation for drivers are some examples of the knowledge areas necessary for managers, the specialised areas depending of course on the particular type of operations carried out by the company.

The manager's knowledge of routing is also important as he is expected to be able to advise drivers on the safest and shortest routes to their destinations. A driver would be annoyed, for example, if he were given a route for his high-sided vehicle which led him towards a low bridge under which he could not pass, causing him to have to reverse out of the situation and back-track onto a different route to complete his journey.

A manager needs to be well educated and many of them possess a qualification of at least O level standard in English language, which is necessary for good report writing and the issuing of written instructions to drivers. He is also expected to have an articulate manner for handling the telephone and must be able to convey precise information to customers and drivers at all times. The transport manager is normally the holder of the Certificate of Professional Competence in his company and he usually has a driving licence which covers the classes of vehicles for which he is responsible.

Employers' associations

Young people just starting their careers in the road transport industry are not likely to be asked about joining employers associations but it is nevertheless interesting to know a little about such associations as they indirectly affect the ways in which companies function. Directors and managers participate in the affairs of associations and this, in turn, affects policy decisions in their companies which may have some effect on the education, training or welfare of young people in the companies. There is a variety of reasons why principals of companies join associations which include, for example, because they feel they ought to, because they feel they need to, or because their involvement confers an aura of respectability and status which will impress some of the people with whom they associate in their professional duties. There are many benefits derived by companies through being members of associations which range from the availability of advice on specific problems which is never more than a telephone call away, to a general appreciation of all an association does for and on behalf of its constituent members. It may, for example, be negotiating with trade unions, through a national joint council, for an increase in wages for apprentices or for compulsory day release for trainees, or it may be lobbying central government on a proposal for a new piece of legislation for road transport.

The Road Haulage Association

The first impression made by the RHA on most young people is usually made by their logo which is displayed on the cab door or the box side of a goods vehicle. The RHA is concerned with the affairs of professional hauliers and consists of many thousands of member companies who operate goods vehicles as a service to trade and industry. There is a number of functional groups within the RHA who specialise in their different areas of interest which include car transporters, bulk liquid, agriculture, caravan haulage, express carriers, heavy haulage, international transport, livestock, long distance, tipping vehicles and waste disposal.

The education and training services the RHA gives to its members include courses and seminars by which advice and assistance can be given to managers, drivers, mechanics and other staff.

The Freight Transport Association

This is an association concerned with trade and industry as operators of road transport vehicles and you may have noticed the FTAs logo displayed in the window of some lorry cabs. The FTA exists to safeguard the interests of, and provide services for, trade and industry as operators and users of freight transport. Member companies range from small business firms that operate one or two vans to large industrial concerns that operate hundreds of vehicles.

The FTA offers a vehicle inspection service to operators and employs a staff of inspectors and engineers who carry out vehicle inspections on trucks and buses. This valuable service provides an independent assessment of the standard of maintenance of vehicles which is useful to operators who are concerned with road safety, vehicle reliability and legal standards which are necessary to meet the requirements of the Department of Transport heavy vehicle tests.

The growth of passenger transport

It is not intended in this book to give a comprehensive coverage of the origins, development and growth of passenger transport as there are already several books available which cover this interesting topic. Very briefly, however, the history of passenger transport started to all intents and purposes in the first quarter of the nineteenth century when horse-drawn buses, owned and operated by individuals, were used to transport fare-paying passengers. Some of these vehicles were single-deckers, others were double-deckers hauled by teams of horses.

Throughout the nineteenth century the number of buses and passengers carried increased as this mode of transport became more popular and a system of licensing, authorised by Act of Parliament, was introduced at the middle of the century. A number of ambitious types of bus were tried out about this time, one of these being a railed system consisting of flat metal rails with a centre guide rail (the latter being used with an additional wheel which kept the vehicle on its flat rail tracks) along which the horse buses would run.

The second half of the nineteenth century witnessed the formation of several partnerships and companies as business continued to prosper and both horse-drawn and steam-propelled trams became popular. Electric trams became more widely used at the turn of the century and this rapidly brought about the demise of horse and steam vehicles.

Some local authorities embarked on municipal ownership of passenger vehicles in the early twentieth century and motor buses, with petrol and diesel engines, emerged during the second decade. For a short period of time up to the 1930s there was fairly continuous expansion of both bus services and tram services, in some instances complementing and in others competing against each other, then the tram services began to decline and by the 1950s most of the trams had been replaced by buses.

In addition to the local authorities that operated passenger transport there were several independent motor bus operators in business from the 1930s who were very enterprising. They opened new routes and, in some cases, creamed off the best of the tramway traffic.

Passenger Transport Authorities

Buses and coaches continued to be operated by municipalities and independent operators up to the late 1960s when the Transport Act 1968 brought about some radical changes by the setting up of the Passenger Transport Authorities (PTAs) and the National Bus Company (NBC). The 1968 Act gave the Transport Minister power to designate any area outside London as a passenger transport area and provide for the creation in each area of a PTA and Passenger

Transport Executive (PTE). The PTAs were initially responsible for co-ordinating the hitherto separate processes of transport planning and land-use planning, and to develop an efficient integrated transport system of road and rail passenger transport. The executive bodies (PTEs) are appointed by the PTAs and are responsible for running the services in their areas. There have been a number of interesting developments brought about by the PTAs which include modern interchange stations where bus and train passengers can change from one mode of transport to the other easily and conveniently.

The National Bus Company NATIONAL

The 1968 Act also brought about the setting up of the NCB which took in existing bus companies which had hitherto operated independently. These included Ribble Motor Services, Midland Red, United Counties, and many others which all operate as subsidiary companies within several regions throughout the country with a headquarters in London. NBC provides healthy competition to both the PTEs and the independent operators by providing a wide range of services for passengers including stage-carriage (local bus services), express services, private hire and excursions. NBC is the largest single bus organisation in the British Isles with some 40 subsidiary undertakings and operating over 20 000 buses and coaches. While economies of scale are derived from the vast national organisation, bureaucratic centralisation is minimised as NBC subsidiary companies are locally based and their operations are largely autonomous. This autonomy has made it possible for the subsidiary companies to retain some of their original identity which existed prior to the 1968 Act.

Express bus and coach operations

There are differences between buses and coaches both in the way the vehicles are designed and in the way they are operated.

Most people regard long distance coach travel as an alternative to rail travel and, as it usually costs less to travel by coach, it is popular. The vehicles used for express coach operations are usually more luxurious than buses by having more comfortable seating, more room, a spacious boot for luggage, toilet facilities on some, and a public address system which can also be used to play music and radio broadcasts. Some passengers prefer coach travel to rail because of its greater flexibility which makes direct door-to-door services possible. Others prefer coaches because the routes that are followed are often more interesting than the rail routes. A further attraction of coach travel is that the luggage is usually much closer to the passenger for the journey. The close proximity of a coach driver also inspires confidence in some passengers as he is more accessible should he be required for any reason.

Express bus and coach drivers are specially trained for the routes they follow and they receive training in luggage handling and passenger relations. The latter is important for carrying senior citizens who need plenty of help with travel information, meal facilities and toilets. There are also a large number of students who use long distance coaches for travelling between home and college or university. Most students have a large amount of luggage, clothing, books and sports equipment, and find that the boot space in a coach is useful for their needs. Drivers are trained to be polite with all groups of passengers, and to dress smartly, as they are their company's ambassadors when on the road. Their training also covers liaison with hotels, coach terminal and airport procedures. A good coach driver develops a sixth sense to cater for the needs of his passengers and by this he can usually anticipate when to stop for a snack, the toilets or the telephones, as well as knowing the right amount of heating and ventilation to keep the passengers comfortable.

Independent operators

In addition to the large PTEs and the NBC there is a large number of independent bus and coach operators both large and small that provide healthy competition for the other public companies and fill the gaps in the passenger transport sector thereby giving a comprehensive transport provision. Many of the independent operators are family businesses and some of them started in a small way with one coach and built up their business, some now owning a large number of vehicles and employing several hundred staff. They operate excursions, school buses, workers' buses, and provide a service for clubs and organisations for trips to the seaside, the countryside, the theatres, and a host of other leisure-time outings.

Drivers are trained in a similar way to bus drivers but they need more knowledge of local or national geography depending on their type of operations. Some are trained additionally to handle vehicle maintenance as it is not always possible to 'ring-in' for assistance or for a replacement vehicle—the one that is broken down may be the only one in the owner's fleet!

Those who work with buses

Most bus people regard themselves as different from truck people as there is less in common between these two sectors today than in any previous period in the history of transport. This has come about mainly as a result of the highly specialised nature of the work in each sector and the consequent need to train people, virtually right from the beginning, to work in one sector or the other.

A *traffic manager* in a bus company, for example, would be responsible to higher management for the efficient and economic operation of bus services in his area, and this includes the supervision and control of platform staff, the inspectorate and the administrative staff under his control. The latter are the people with the detailed knowledge of routing, one-way streets and building programmes in the operating area.

A *transport engineer's* responsibilities are also slightly different from his counterpart in the road haulage sector. He is responsible for the preparation and maintenance of programmes and records for the servicing, maintenance, repair and overhaul of vehicles. He has to ensure that buses are prepared and are up to standard for the renewing of PSV Annual Licences and the PSV Certificate of Fitness examinations. He is also expected to monitor strictly and to quantify all matters related to the fuel consumed by his fleet of vehicles. This is important because of the high cost of fuel for bus operations and the growing scarcity of fuels. He also needs to liaise with vehicle manufacturers on the design features of vehicles, and his advice is invaluable to designers on such matters as type of vehicle suspension to be used, the layout of the seating, number of doors and step heights. Further to his engineering responsibilities he needs some knowledge of work study, statistics and labour relations as some of his time will be taken up in discussion and negotiation with trade unions.

The duties of *drivers* also differ in some ways from those of a truck driver. There is usually much more stopping and starting, a need to attend to passengers, and an ability to cope with driving in high traffic densities through cities and towns for a large proportion of their driving time. To make the latter a little easier for drivers local authorities have made provision for bus lanes on general purpose roads and these are reserved for buses only. It is an offence for other vehicles to enter these lanes when they are in operation which is usually during peak hours. These lanes are clearly marked with special signs which indicate the time of operation.

The vehicles

The vintage and veterans

If you talk to some of the more elderly people in the truck and bus industry they will be able to tell you many stories about their experiences with the vehicles of the past. Some of those vehicles were not fitted with electric starter motors, as all are today, and starting up on a cold and frosty morning was often a great ordeal. Many of the old trucks and buses had a starting handle permanently fixed and dangling at the front which was the only means tht drivers had of starting up their engines. Some of the old diesel-engined trucks were fitted with a decompressor lever alongside the starting handle which the driver had to operate with one hand whilst 'swinging' the starting handle with the other. This usually worked if the engine was warm but was seldom any use when cold. A thick piece of rope was therefore carried on these vehicles for use when starting up from cold. The rope was tied to the handle and help was needed from colleagues who would assist the driver on the handle by all tugging on the rope (just like a tug of war game) and, after several snatches of the rope, the engine would start. Some of the old engines required 'priming' before attempting to start them from cold and this was done by operating the priming levers on the fuel injection pump which forced fuel into the engine cylinders thereby providing an excess amount of diesel fuel which aided the initial starting.

Heavy overcoats, boots or clogs, gloves and caps were worn by most drivers in cold weather as cab heating was not provided as it is in today's trucks and buses. Drivers had to rely on the heat from the engine to keep them warm and this was not easily controllable, often resulting in being too warm in summer and too cold in winter. Power-assisted steering and semi- or fully-automatic transmission systems and power brakes were not fitted on trucks and buses of the past which meant that drivers had to be physically fit enough to handle their vehicles. Traffic densities were not normally as high in cities and towns as they are today which meant that these aids were not as important as they are today, but the older trucks and buses, by virtue of being harder to handle, caused more strain and fatigue on drivers.

Today's vehicles

If you are considering making trucks and buses your future career you will no doubt already be interested in the vehicles themselves. If you have not taken a particular interest up to now, then it is time to start and this simply means keeping your eyes open when you are around and about as it is difficult to go anywhere without seeing trucks and buses.

Trucks

You will no doubt have realised by now that trucks have to be more heavily constructed than motor cars so that they are strong enough to carry payloads for the operator. There are many different shapes, sizes and designs of trucks depending on the particular type of operation for which it is being used.

Rigid vehicles

The rigid vehicle is the conventional type of truck which was developed from the motor car and has two axles and four wheels, although there are often double wheels on the rear axle. Even though the total number of wheels is six, these vehicles are still referred to as four-wheeled. If you look out for rigid vehicles you will sooner or later notice that some have three axles and others have four. Those trucks with three axles are known as six-wheeled and normally have two axles at the rear and one at the front, although there are some with two axles at the front giving four steered wheels. These vehicles are sometimes known as a Chinese Six. The four-axled rigid vehicles have two driving axles at the rear and two axles at the front which carry the steered wheels. These trucks have a total of twelve wheels but they are referred to in the road transport industry as eight-wheeled.

Truck recognition

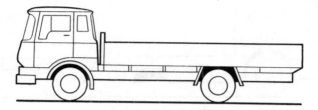

(a) The four-wheeled flat truck with drop sides is popular amongst many operators who operate as road hauliers and carriers

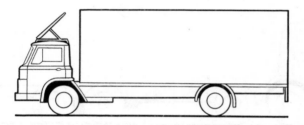

(b) The box van, sometimes fitted with an air deflector on the cab roof, is often used for carrying food or furniture

(c) The skip truck is a special purpose vehicle designed for a particular type of operation and cannot normally be used for other types of operation

57

Trucks

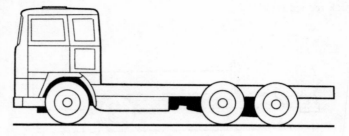

(d) This six-wheeled rigid chassis (vehicle without body) is one of the heavier range of trucks

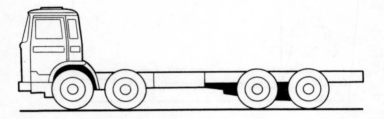

(e) The eight-wheeled rigid chassis has the advantage of twin-steered wheels which makes it easier to handle when being driven in confined spaces

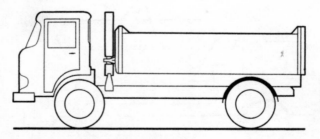

(f) The tipper truck, a common sight on many roads, is usually a short wheel-base vehicle

(g)Used for carrying fuels such as diesel and petrol are tankers like this one

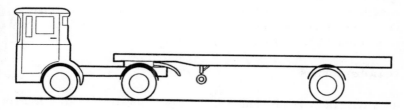

(h)Very popular amongst transport operators is the articulated vehicle which consists of a tractor unit and semi-trailer

(i)The rigid truck with a draw-bar trailer is not as common nowadays as it used to be but there are some of these combinations being operated

Trucks

Articulated vehicles

These vehicles can easily be recognised by their two distinct parts joined by a coupling, the front portion being known as the tractor or tractive unit and the rear portion known as the semi-trailer. These vehicles are very popular with many transport operators as they are more manoeuvrable than a rigid vehicle of similar length which makes them more easy to handle in a confined space as their turning circle is smaller. Another advantage of articulated vehicles to the operator is that a number of semi-trailers can be used with one tractor unit which sometimes makes operations more economical as the unit and the driver can be working for longer periods than would be possible with only one trailer. Two disadvantages of articulated trucks are that they are more difficult to reverse than rigid vehicles and they are more difficult to handle in adverse weather conditions when, for instance, there is snow and ice on the roads. Drivers are therefore specially trained to handle these trucks and need a Class 1 HGV Driving Licence to drive them.

Draw-bar trailers

This type of trailer is similar in its basic construction to a four-wheeled rigid vehicle but it does not have its own engine and transmission system. It is connected to the drawing vehicle by its draw-bar and the trailer's front axle is pivoted so that it can turn and steer the trailer in the path of the drawing vehicle.

Drivers find draw-bar trailers are slightly more easy to handle than semi-trailers of articulated vehicles even though the combined length of the vehicle and trailer is often longer than an articulated outfit.

An advantage of draw-bar trailers to operators is that they can be used when the occasion warrants it. If a pay load can be carried on the truck alone the trailer can be left at the depot. On the other hand, if a pay load is too bulky or too heavy for the truck, the trailer may be brought into operation. This is more economical than would be the case if the driver and truck had to make two separate journeys, or two drivers and vehicles had to be used to shift the same load.

Are heavier and bigger trucks likely?

For several years now, some operators have argued that they could compete on more equal terms with their foreign counterparts if they were allowed to operate heavier and bigger trucks. The maximum gross weight of trucks, allowed by law in Britain, is approximately 32.5 tonnes (32 ton) whereas some of the trucks operated by overseas countries are considerably heavier. There are of course arguments against, as well as for, heavier trucks in Britain which means that it could be some considerable time, and perhaps never, before heavier trucks are permitted.

Operators see heavier trucks as being more efficient and more economical as an increased pay load could be carried. Most drivers would also agree to driving these trucks but many of them would expect a higher rate of pay to cover the increased responsibility of handling them. But, on the other hand, there are many people who object to heavier and bigger trucks for a number of reasons. Some argue that heavier trucks will cause a more rapid deterioration in the condition of the motorways and roads, others fear that more damage will be caused to buildings, particularly old ones which are in narrow streets, by the vibrations from the vehicles. Others feel that they will be frightened, and even terrified, when travelling on the motorways in their cars if they are overtaken by heavier high-speed trucks. Others think that heavier trucks will be noisier and more smokey although transport engineers have already dispelled this theory and some engineers go as far as to claim that they can actually reduce noise and exhaust smoke levels below those that are tolerated at the present time—but their claims will be more costly to implement.

So only time will tell whether larger trucks will be operated on our roads and we will have to wait and see. In the meantime we will have to be satisfied with studying the possibilities that we may see in future years if legislation is changed and one such possibility is the 'double bottom'.

Double bottom road trains

If heavier goods vehicles are permitted in the future then the 'double bottom' is one possibility. This outfit is a combination of an articulated vehicle and a draw-bar trailer which increases the load-carrying capacity and makes a bigger pay load possible.

The double bottom is designed from the outset as a vehicle for long-distance motorway operations and would not be suitable (or acceptable by many people) for driving through the streets of towns and villages. It is therefore likely, if double bottoms are ever permitted, that terminals will be built at strategic points where motorways link with cities and towns so that these vehicles can pull in at the terminals and their trailers can be uncoupled. Two relatively light tractor units could then be employed, one taking the semi-trailer and the other taking the draw-bar trailer with its front axle removed, to run the trailers into the nearby town and deliver the goods. Following delivery, a new load could be picked up and taken back to the terminal by the lighter trucks where the double bottom would be waiting to take back the trailers and start off again on its long-distance journey. A highly organised company operating double bottoms and a fleet of lighter tractor units could no doubt operate a long-distance trunk and shunt service which would be profitable.

Drivers would have to be specially trained to handle double bottoms as they are not only heavier and longer than conventional trucks but are virtually impossible to reverse. Whether a modified Class 1 HGV Driving Licence would be sufficient to drive these vehicles or whether a new Class of licence would have to be introduced remains to be seen.

Truck cabs

If you eventually become a HGV driver you will spend a large amount of your working time in a vehicle cab as do all drivers. It is important therefore that cabs are designed for maximum comfort and safety and designers put a great deal of thought and effort into cab design and development by striving to make the cab suit the driver. Some of the important points that go into cab design, apart from individual styling, are provision for maximum vision and comfort, and easy access to all the controls. Designers aim for armchair comfort in the cab so that drivers can feel fairly relaxed and comfortable behind the wheel. The seating has to be adjustable so that it suits fat and thin, and long and short legged drivers, and the heating system and air conditioning has to be easy to adjust so that the driver can be warm in winter and cool in summer, with provision of fresh air at all times, as a stuffy atmosphere can cause drowsiness and reduce safety standards.

As most cabs are built and located over the engines in trucks there needs to be ample lagging (insulation) around the engine compartment to minimise noise levels for the driver whilst, at the same time, the engine needs to be easily accessible for repairs and maintenance. Some cabs are made from sheet steel, others are built with glass-reinforced-plastic panels, the latter giving lightness but less resistance to impact. There is also an increasing number of vehicles being built with tilt-cabs which are useful when access to the engine is needed.

The driver's seat is positioned to give him a panoramic view through the windows with the windows themselves being designed to give as good a view as possible. Some vehicles have extremely low windows, others have low corner windows, both designs being employed to give the driver the best view possible. The controls and instruments in a modern truck appear very complicated to many people, and remind some of an aircraft cockpit, as there are many gauges, warning lights and buzzers, switches and numerous controls which take some understanding. An HGV driver's training includes the use and familiarisation of these instruments and controls and a good driver makes use of all of them, although not all at the same time.

There are an increasing number of trucks being built with sleeper cabs, these having bunk beds fitted which are useful for long-distance operations. These trucks will no doubt be useful in the future if there is an increase in overseas operations.

Buses

Passenger vehicles—buses and coaches

The buses of earlier times were built along conventional lines with their bodies mounted on separate chassis frames and their engines, which were powered by either petrol or diesel fuel, were front mounted. Some of the early double-deck models can be seen in transport museums and it will be noticed that they were often built with an open rear staircase and an open top deck. Later designs did away with the open versions, and staircases and upper decks were enclosed in the interest of passenger safety and comfort. The open rear platform for the passengers to board and alight remained a standard feature for many years after the other enclosures were implemented and a conductor (guard) was employed to ensure safety of passengers as they boarded and alighted, and to collect their fares.

Buses

There have been many different designs of double-deck buses over the past years, one interesting development being the low bridge version which was specially designed for companies which operated vehicles in districts where there were low tunnels and bridges. These buses could easily be recognised by their side gangway on the upper deck together with bench type seats to accommodate four passengers on each. This layout enabled the body designers to plan the overall height of the buses several centimetres lower than was possible with the conventional layout, and this made all the difference between the vehicle being able to pass through a tunnel or not.

Single-deck buses of bygone years were usually designed to suit both urban operations and long-distance express tours. The only differences, if any, were the availability of a choice of rear axle gear ratios, different strengths of road springs, and a different tuning recommendation for the engine.

Today's buses and coaches, however, are very different from those of bygone years. The larger variety of operating conditions and the changes in the nature of operations in more recent years has led to many different designs and sizes of vehicles being built to suit the type of operation which range from the commuter city bus to the long-distance motorway express.

The number of doorways in modern buses also vary depending on their type of operation. A bus designed for urban operations is usually built with two, and sometimes three, doorways so that passengers can quickly and easily board and alight, whereas a long-distance coach may only have one doorway. Most city buses are designed as one-man-operated vehicles and are fitted with fare collecting boxes and ticket-issuing machines at the entrance where passengers can pay their fares and receive a ticket or punch their clipper cards. Doorways at the front, or at the front and the middle, are obviously safer for passengers who travel on one-man-operated buses than would be the case if the doorway was at the rear.

If you want to train as a craftsman and not as a driver you will learn the different types of vehicle construction during your training. One of the first things you will learn is the way that vehicles are built up from scratch. In the early days buses were built by fitting a separate body to a chassis. Nowadays the chassis frame and body are often built as one integral unit with all the members and panels being fixed together with rivets, or by welding, in preference to the

64

Bus recognition

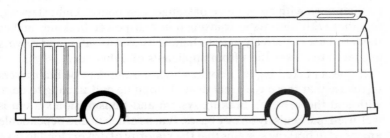

(a) The two-door rear-engined single deck bus is very popular and operated
by many Passenger Transport Authorities and the National
Bus Company

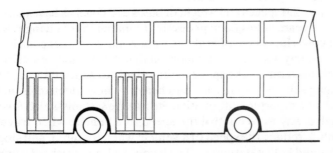

(b) The double decker is used extensively in the United Kingdom but they
are not as popular overseas

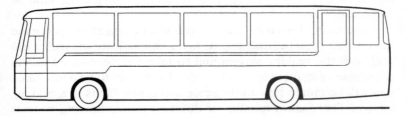

(c) The coach is designed for long distance operations and has fewer doors
than a bus. It has more comfortable seating and is fitted out
with more luxuries

older method of using nuts and bolts.

Most drivers like the newer buses because they are much easier to handle with their power-assisted steering which makes them light to steer even with 50 or more passengers on board. Light steering, together with automatic transmission and power braking, makes modern buses relatively easy to handle as well as safer, and drivers are recruited these days from applicants of either sex.

It doesn't take long for people who are training to be bus drivers to realise that there is a great deal of stopping and starting to cope with and the vehicle's braking system and transmission system is well used, particularly on city buses. But, so efficient and dependable are modern braking systems that the majority of drivers tend to take them for granted. Even though this is largely true, the braking system of any vehicle should not be taken for granted as it is extremely important in terms of road safety for drivers, craftsmen, passengers and all other road users alike.

As the road speeds and weight of buses and coaches have increased over the years, it has been necessary to match these changes with a more powerful system of braking. Brakes make a direct contribution to road safety and it is most important that they should be sufficiently powerful to control the speed of the vehicle to which they are fitted. Training schemes for drivers and heavy vehicle mechanics include useful and important information on braking systems which function in such a way as to control the speed of a vehicle when travelling downhill, reduce the speed of a vehicle when required, and stop the vehicle and hold it stationary. The layout and equipment of a braking system varies with each type and make of bus and coach, and systems are usually more sophisticated on heavier vehicles than on lighter ones, but the functions of the systems remain the same in each case.

If you train to become *a driver* you will be taught to appreciate the warnings that the instruments in the cab indicate when all is not well with the braking system and to take the necessary steps in consequence in the interest of safety. If you train to be *a mechanic* you will be taught how to diagnose and repair faults in a braking system. There are a number of different power braking systems used on buses and coaches, two of the most common being operated by air pressure or hydraulic pressure. Air brakes operate by a complex system of valves, pipes and pressure tanks, and when the driver presses the brake pedal he is really operating a system of valves which permit compressed air to actuate pistons in cylinders on the vehicle's axles which operate the brakes.

Coaches

Coaches are similar in construction to single-deck buses but are designed to be more luxurious and tend to have a heavier body. Coaches normally seat between 28 and 53 passengers and are designed from the outset for long-distance journeys which sometimes span overnight. The vehicles are built with a spacious boot and ample luggage lockers, comfortable seating, window curtains, adequate heating and air-conditioning, soft lighting, radio and tape music and a public address system. Some are additionally equipped with toilet facilities and a cocktail bar. Coach engines may be mounted at the front, the rear, or in the middle, the latter design sometimes incorporating a horizontally mounted engine which reduces any obstructive hump in the saloon which may have to be tolerated with a vertically mounted power unit.

Truck and bus engines

It is possible to receive education and training to specialise in engine repairs and overhauls which some people find very interesting and there are companies where a career can be taken up as a diesel engine fitter.

An interesting point about the engines used in some trucks and buses is that they are not of the same manufacture as the vehicle itself. For many years there have been a number of engine builders who have supplied engines for trucks and buses. In some cases it has always been possible, and still is, for an operator who orders a vehicle from a manufacturer to specify the make and model of engine he would like fitted in his vehicle, and the vehicle manufacturer will oblige if possible. Vehicles which are built and supplied this way are more expensive than those which are purchased off-the-shelf as standard-built trucks or buses, but operators have the satisfaction of knowing that their vehicles are matched to their particular types of operations if they have been built to their own specifications.

Starting your new job

The first day at work is usually found to be a bewildering experience and seldom gives a real impression of what the future is really going to be like. The excitement of going into a working situation for the first time and earning a wage can give you a new feeling of independence and make you feel as if you have suddenly grown up into an important person. You have indeed become important in the sense that you are part of a team of people with a joint responsibility for the operation of a number of trucks or buses and your contribution, small as it may be initially, is still important. You suddenly find yourself mixing with a new group of people which contains a larger proportion of adults than any group in which you will have previously been involved, and the earlier time of starting in the morning all make for a tiring and exhausting day.

It usually pays to be humble during the first few weeks in your new job if you don't want to be called 'Big head' by the others working with you. Remember that it is easy to enter into new employment with a little knowledge of the job and although this is not necessarily a bad thing it may easily be taken by other people in the group as a 'cocky attitude' on your part if you overplay your role and may lead to you becoming a little unpopular. Human nature being what it is, an experienced craftsman or manager does not usually like to be told by a newcomer that his techniques and methods are out-of-date (even though some of them may be!) so be tactful and discreet during your early days by allowing yourself to integrate slowly into the new group and you will gradually be accepted as a welcome colleague.

In a different sense it will be expected that you show some initiative and you can demonstrate some of your confidence by asking politely some questions about the new job and trying hard to carry out each allotted task to the best of your ability. Try to keep on good terms with your colleagues. A big-headed attitude on the one hand or an obvious lack of interest on the other can adversely affect relationships with the other people in the group.

Be prepared for tricks that may be played on you by some of the more senior people. If you are a craftsman's apprentice you may be asked to go to the tool store for a 'glass hammer' and if you are a trainee clerk you may be sent to the traffic office for a 'long stand'. Admittedly, some of these tricks help you to become familiar with your new company but they can be a little annoying at the time they are tried on.

Try to be as co-operative as possible with your superiors. A willingness to do your best, even under arduous conditions, is usually appreciated even though this may not at the time be apparent. Try to be punctual and reliable by arriving regularly on time both in the morning and at lunchtime. Don't let the game of football or cards at lunchtime drag on for too long and so make you late back, or the boss will almost certainly become annoyed with you. Try to develop good clean habits at work—wash your hands before mid-day breaks, keep your cup clean, don't let your overalls or smocks get too dirty before changing them for clean ones. If you don't change your protective clothing regularly don't be surprised if you pick-up the nickname 'grease monkey'.

If you are irregular and unpunctual in your habits at work your boss will lose confidence in you. If, for example, you are working on a rush job on a vehicle that is wanted as soon as possible for service and you are either late in or not present at all to deal with the job, your boss will be most annoyed—and quite rightly so. Remember that he has a responsibility to his superiors in the same way that you have a responsibility to him, and if a vehicle is prevented from being turned out because you have not carried out your part of the job appertaining to the vehicle then your superiors are not going to be very impressed are they?

When working with trucks and buses it is sometimes necessary to stay on at work after the normal finishing time. An extra half-hour may be needed to finish off a job so that a vehicle can go on to the road. Remember, a vehicle that is parked in its garage is not earning its keep. It has to be on the road before there is any chance of making a profit for the company, and if you are the person who is responsible for keeping the vehicle off the road then you are not going to be popular with your superiors. Although you will only have a small amount of responsibility at first, this small amount must be understood and accepted by yourself as it is an important small beginning.

Fewer and fewer truck and bus companies are training their young people by simply letting them start work without any direct supervision. Being left alone to pick up a job in the best way possible is slow, costly to the company, and inefficient to both parties. And further to this, an apprentice or trainee who is given the menial tasks at the beginning of his career such as cleaning up or running errands for most of the time quickly gets bored and loses interest. The vast majority of companies today have accepted that good training for their staff pays off, even though this may be in the long term, and most managers and directors insist that young people, who are just entering their companies, be formally and systematically trained. Details of training for some of the various jobs in the truck and bus industry are explained on pages 84 to 94.

Your wage

Most young people in the road transport industry are paid weekly. If you are starting a new job, however, you may not receive any wage during your first week as you may be working a week-in-hand. In such a case your first pay packet would be given to you during your second week. The advantage of the week-in-hand system is to the employer who is given more time to work out the wages with the various deductions (stoppages) which lead to a considerable difference between a person's gross and net wage. The amount of money you receive in your wage is stated on a wage slip which is a document stating your gross and net wage with the deductions itemised. The slip or statement is usually given to you before you actually receive the money or it is given at the same time as the money by being enclosed in a transparent packet so that it can easily be read. As an apprentice or trainee your wage is usually calculated on an hourly basis. This means that you are paid for each hour you work and the total number of hours you work in a week are added up and multiplied by the hourly rate to give your total gross wage. Added to this there may be a bonus payment, if your company operates a bonus system, and there may be some overtime payment at a higher hourly rate if you have worked extra hours in the week.

National Insurance

When your wage reaches a certain level you will be liable for statutory deductions which consist of National Insurance and Income Tax deductions. These stoppages can make a big difference to your net (take home pay) wage and be somewhat of a disappointment to young people. However, some of your National Insurance contributions cover such things as unemployment, sickness, injury at work, retirement and widows pensions, chest X rays, and a number of other benefits of which any of us may, and in most cases will, sooner or later take advantage.

Income Tax
Your Income Tax contribution is also statutory, this means that it is required by law, and you have no other option but to pay your dues. The taxation system of payment is known as Pay-As-You-Earn (PAYE) and the amount of money you owe the Inland Revenue is deducted from your wage each time you are paid. This method of payment is regarded by the majority of people as the least painless as it follows the saying 'What you never have you never miss'.

Trade Unions

When you start your new job you may be asked to join a trade union or workers' association. Whether you will, or will not, be asked to join depends on the particular company for which you are working as union involvement varies between companies. In some companies every single worker is expected to be a member of a union, in others it is left to each individual whether he or she joins, and there are a few companies where there are no union members at all.

Unions also provide facilities for education and training of their members by making available correspondence courses, weekend schools and college scholarships.

Transport and General Workers' Union (T & GWU)

The history of trade unions is very interesting, particularly those who have transport workers in their membership, and you will have no doubt studied a little about the birth and development of unions in your history lessons at school.

The T & GWU nowadays links goods and passenger transport with some of the new growth industries and it includes many people with various types of skills in administration, clerical, technical and supervisory capacities in its numerous trade groups and sections.

Amalgamated Union of Engineering Workers

The AUEW is a prominent member of the National Joint Council for the Motor Vehicle Retail and Repair Industry and there is a vast number of engineers, technicians, craftsmen and others in membership.

There is a Junior Section in the AUEW made up of young people who work in the industry and each year they meet together at the Union's annual conference for junior workers to discuss suggestions for improving matters in industry and obtaining higher standards of living for young workers.

Apprentice craftsmen and technicians

Before starting work on a vehicle

There are a number of disciplines that should be carried out before starting a job on a truck or bus and these will be fully explained to you during the early part of your training. The first thing to remember is that personal cleanliness is very important and you should do all that is possible to protect yourself from injuries and diseases when at work. Working on trucks and buses is often a dirty task and it is important that you wear clothing that is serviceable and gives protection. Boiler suits are normally preferred to dust coats as when wearing the latter there is always a tendency for your trousers to be splashed with fuel, oil or grease. It is also necessary to have more than one boiler suit as this will need regular cleaning and repairing.

As protective clothing cannot be worn to cover your body completely some of your skin will be exposed when working and a hand barrier cream should be used to protect your skin. This will repel particular irritants by acting as a separator between your skin and the irritant and will also make hand washing easier after a working session. Barrier creams reduce the risk of catching industrial skin diseases due to dermatitis—this being an irritation or inflammation of the skin caused by some irritating substance met with while at work. Contact with oil, grease, resin and solvents are just a few substances which can cause dermatitis and, although not contagious, usually needs medical treatment to cure.

It is also important that you have suitable footwear for comfort and protection. No sensible mechanic would wear soft plimsolls or sandals in a garage. What is required is a pair of substantial shoes or boots especially made for industrial use and these are usually made with steel toe caps fitted internally which reduce the risk of injury to the toes should a component or tool be accidentally dropped. Rubber soles are ideal when working on electrical components. Some mechanics wear safety helmets when working beneath a vehicle. These protect your head against falling dirt, rust, components and tools, and also help to keep fuel, oil and grease out of your hair.

It is not uncommon to see goggles being worn by garage staff. These give protection to your eyes when drilling and grinding, or when removing dirt, rust and scale from vehicle components.

Garages differ considerably in their facilities for personal washing and cleaning up after work. In some workshops a washbasin, soap

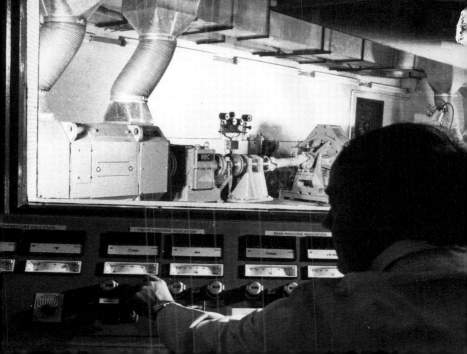

and towel may be all that is supplied while other garages are equipped with hot air driers, showers and changing rooms which make it possible to have a thorough clean-up and change of clothing after work. This is handy if you are to attend an appointment immediately after leaving your workplace and can particularly apply to apprentices who have to attend evening classes at college.

Garage tools for apprentice mechanics

A vehicle mechanic without tools is as much use in his job as a pupil without a pen, pencil and sheet of writing paper. Tools are essential for doing jobs on vehicles and there is virtually no maximum limit to the number of tools that a mechanic should possess. Apprentices usually build up their tool kits over a period of time and there are several ways of collecting tools. One method, though not too common, is for the company initially to supply freely all the tools necessary for the job and replace any that break or wear. Another method which is much harder on the apprentice's pocket is for him to buy all the tools himself that are necessary to do the work. Another way, and this is quite common, is for the apprentice to purchase tools from his employer by paying for them by weekly deductions from his wage. This system has the advantage of a slightly lower purchasing price to the apprentice made possible by the employer buying the tools in bulk in the first instance. A further advantage of this scheme to the apprentice is that he does not miss the money that he pays for his tools in this way as much as he would if he were paying for tools from wages he had already received. A mechanic's tools are usually kept in a tool box or a tool chest which is mounted on casters so that it can easily be moved around the workshop. A plentiful kit of tools can cost hundreds of pounds and it takes most people a long time to acquire a comprehensive kit. Once you have collected your own kit together it is advisable to take out insurance cover against loss or damage as it would be heartbreaking to have to start collecting all over again if they were lost.

The craftsman and technician in the truck and bus industry differs in a number of ways from the craftsmen in other trades and not least in the tools and equipment he requires to do his job. A house painter and decorator for example requires far less equipment to do his job than a vehicle mechanic.

73

Training and further education

The College of Further Education

If you think you have finished with classroom work once you leave school you may well be in for a shock as there is likely to be a good deal more classroom study required from you in the years which lie ahead. It is almost certain that you will spend some of your future studying time in an institute of further education which may be an Institute of Technology, a College of Technology, a College of Further Education, a Technical College, or some other similar title, and there is a vast range of courses offered by colleges for young people who are pursuing a career in the truck and bus industry. The person in charge of a college is known as the 'principal' and his job is not unlike that of a general manager's in a large transport company. The college principal's name is usually stated on all official written communications such as letters, press notices, the college prospectus and so on, although most students have little personal contact with him whilst attending courses at a college. The principal is assisted by a vice-principal and a chief administrative officer, the latter being concerned with the matters related to enrolment, registration and examination entries for students as well as being the boss of the college office.

Colleges are divided into a number of departments, each with a 'head', and students who are employed in the truck and bus industry are likely to study in the engineering department if they are taking courses for qualifying as craftsmen or technicians, and are likely to be studying in the management and business studies department if pursuing a course in transport management. A head does not do much lecturing in his department, his main duties being more of an administrative type, although he is responsible for the academic standards of the work done in his department and he invariably

74

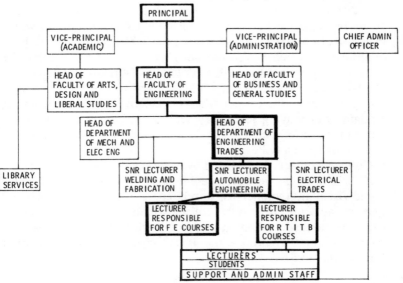

Organisation of a technical college

takes a great deal of interest in matters such as examination results, attendance of students during their courses, and the type and suitability of courses being offered to students. The head is the person who is responsible for timetabling his staff to classes, making sure that students are placed on the best course for themselves, and seeing that attendance registers and students' reports are maintained and kept up to date.

College lecturers

The people who you will have most contact with whilst studying at a college are the lecturers who spend most of their college time in classrooms, workshops and laboratories assisting students during their learning. Most college departments are divided into sections or units and each section is headed by a principal lecturer or a senior lecturer. An apprentice heavy vehicle mechanic, for example, would take a course in an automobile engineering section of a college whilst a trainee traffic manager would probably take a course in a college's organisational studies unit.

College lecturers are highly qualified people and have mastered

75

two different types of professional skills, one resulting in the achievement of a technical or commercial qualification gained whilst in industry or business, the other being the achievement of a teacher's qualification which is also normally gained prior to entering the lecturing profession. You will no doubt have already thought about the basic difference between a secondary school teacher and a college lecturer, the former who is normally trained for teaching straight after leaving secondary school and university whilst the latter takes a job in industry or commerce between leaving school and lecturing in a college.

College lecturers are assisted by other people known as 'support staff' who may be workshop technicians, laboratory technicians, audio-visual aid technicians, storekeepers or clerk/typists who all play an important role in the college which houses a great deal of expensive and sophisticated equipment which needs to be stored, maintained and repaired so that it is always in good working order for students to use.

Industrial training and the Training Boards

The Industrial Training Act of 1964 brought about major changes in the opportunities and methods used for training, and the truck and bus industry has been very actively involved with training since this Act was passed.

The purpose of providing training for trainees is to induce expertise which will enable them to undertake tasks in their industry which include the mastery of skills and techniques acquired during the training period. Training may be given to trainees by their employers whilst in the company and doing their job of work, or it may be given at a company's training school, or at a group training centre, or at a Board approved college. There are of course differences in approach and long term objectives between these ways of training. It needs to be borne in mind that the companies that provide their own training in their premises known as 'on the job training' are, with the very best intentions, going to be biased in their training aims by company policy and its aims. This does not necessarily mean that company training is inferior to the other ways but it does mean it is different.

On the other hand, training which is provided by a college for example, known as 'off the job training', is not influenced by such

76

pressures as company policy or profit motives and training does not take second place to pressing emergencies that tend to occur from time to time in a company. 'Off the job' training being divorced from the actual working situation has the advantage of being a more concentrated form of training aimed at achieving high standards of skills and techniques.

The Road Transport Industrial Training Board (RTITB)

This Board has a great deal of influence on the training given to most people in the truck and bus industry. The board comprises members drawn from employers in the industry, trade union members, educationalists and other people concerned with, or interested in, training and its scope covers the road haulage sector and passenger transport sector of the industry as well as several others which include car mechanics and motor cycle mechanics. The Board has its own training centres, two of which are known as Motecs (Multi-occupational Training and Education Centres) through which several thousands of people in the truck and bus industry have already passed, and it is very likely that the vast majority of young people entering this industry will, at some time in their career, attend a training board centre or establishment for some aspect of training. The two well known RTITB Motecs are situated at High Ercall near Shrewsbury and Livingstone in Scotland where hundreds of apprentices and trainees have attended a wide variety of courses which include training for vehicle servicing and repairs, welding, furniture removal, bus driving and conducting, HGV driving, fork-lift truck operating, supervising and managing, and driving instruction. The Livingstone centre is purpose built and young people who attend are made to feel comfortable during their stay which may be for only one or two days or several weeks. It is well equipped with some of the best vehicles and equipment that are available for training and, as 'all work and no play makes Jack a dull boy', it also has ample recreational, sports and social facilities including badminton, a gymnasium, squash courts, swimming pool, table tennis, snooker, darts and football. Television lounges and cinema shows are also provided at both Motecs.

Initial training and re-training

The training you will receive in the truck and bus industry is likely to be in two or more parts. Your initial training, which you will receive early in your career, will consist mainly of a basic preparation which includes skills and knowledge necessary to progress in your career. Additionally, you are likely to receive further training throughout your career in the industry which will be necessary for you to keep up to date with future developments of a technical and commercial nature that will inevitably take place. Initial training is often in the form of an apprenticeship and is received during a young person's early years in the industry, which consists mainly of training to acquire the basic skills and techniques together with the associated further education related to the job where the skills will be applied. Companies invest an enormous amount of money in initial training for their young people as they see this as a long term investment which will benefit the company as well as the trainee in future years. Most initial training is frequently monitored by employers and training board officers to ensure that an acceptable standard is reached and maintained throughout the whole training period. Records of progress and attainment are made during the training period and skill tests are often included at stages throughout the training period

It is not uncommon for people to attend periodically courses of re-training throughout their careers. Most vehicle and component manufacturers, for example, provide courses of training for companies on current developments and new products. Many companies take advantage of these courses by sending some of their staff along to up-date their knowledge and skills which will be of benefit to both the person attending the course and to the company. There are likely to be more of these courses in the future as technology is progressing at a faster and faster rate and it becomes more and more important for staff to keep pace with these changes. Courses for re-training are usually provided in a purpose built training school staffed by experienced and qualified instructors and the courses cover the operation, servicing and fault diagnosis of products including the use and knowledge of special tools, test benches and fitting techniques. Though most of these courses are for a short duration there is usually a test or examination at the end of the course and the results, which may be of a practical and/or a theory test, are usually passed on to the trainees employer.

College courses

Colleges offer a wide range of courses suitable for all age groups in the truck and bus industry. The pattern and level of courses vary widely depending upon the particular type of course, and it sometimes pays to shop around the colleges in your area before making a decision and enroling, as there are slight variations in course duration, course content and quality of college equipment and these are worth considering before you make up your mind. Most colleges publish their prospectus of courses prior to the beginning of each academic year and leaflets on short and special courses are normally available on request from the college registrar. One point worth bearing in mind is that there may be restrictions which do not permit students to attend a college outside the area in which they reside. These restrictions are imposed by local education authorities for certain courses and, provided an authority offers a course at one of its colleges, will not normally permit a student resident in its area to take up a similar course in a college in a neighbouring authority's area.

Day release courses

A substantial number of students who are employed in the truck and bus industry are granted time out of work to attend college for one day in each week of the academic year. This is commonly known as the day release system and is very popular with employers who, in most cases, pay the wages to their student/employee for the day that he attends college. Most employers qualify for a training grant from their training board which helps them to support their employees during the time they are attending college. The day release system is obviously an advantage to a student when compared with the older system of part-time evening study which used to exist and involved attendance at college on two or three evenings in each week for several years to obtain a qualification. There are still many mature, experienced and successful people in the truck and bus industry who hold positions of responsibility who started their careers by working six days in each week and attending evening classes in addition. However, those days have gone forever, but they are not forgotten by some of the people who were brought up in this era, and you will no doubt hear more about the 'old days' as you progress through your career.

College courses

Day release courses, though quite common, have their disadvantages to employers and employees. As far as the employer is concerned the daily work cycle is interrupted during the temporary absence of staff attending college and this may cause vehicles to be off the road for a longer period of time than would be the case if the staff were continuously present. As far as young people are concerned, their day at the 'tech' can seem a long day as they are on the premises for a long period of time, a typical day being from nine in the morning to seven or later in the evening. Although the total hours in classes are not always more than the hours of attendance at the workplace they seem much longer to some students as they are more restricted to classrooms and workshops and, in many cases, are less physically active than when in their normal workplace. There is also the possibility of having to attend college on an additional evening between say, seven and nine, to cope with the curriculum work of some courses and to comply with the regulations regarding the hours of attendance necessary for satisfactory completion of the course. In addition, there is also college work which has to be done at home which may take the form of supplementary reading, writing up projects or laboratory work reports, doing set work as directed by the lecturers, or revising work and tackling exercises as preparation for phase tests or end-of-course examinations.

Part-time day release courses usually last for four or five years and many of them are designed to complement the apprenticeship or trainee training of young people. The normal starting age for day release courses is 16, although there are some exceptions to this, and completion of the courses is timed to coincide with the completion of the young person's apprenticeship which is normally between 20 and 21 when he becomes recognised as a fully skilled person in his occupation and drawing the full rate of pay for his work.

Other courses in colleges

From what you have already read in this book you will have gathered that colleges have a long tradition of providing courses for people in road transport as well as in many other fields. The origins of colleges can be traced back to the earlier Mechanics Institutes where many of the country's greatest engineers and scientists received their early education and developed their ideas. The majority of managers and engineers of today also received some of their further education

80

in colleges, and this trend is very likely to continue for those in the truck and bus industry for many years to come. In addition to the part-time day release courses which have already been explained there are several other types of course available in colleges, two of the most common being full-time and block release courses which have some advantages to both employers and students when compared with day release courses.

Full-time courses

Full-time courses are offered by colleges to a fairly wide age group of young people, starting with courses that are suitable for school leavers and ranging to more advanced courses for students who wish to pursue their studies for professional qualifications. Courses for school leavers include foundation courses, first-year diploma courses, and pre-apprenticeship courses some of which are designed with a definite vocational bias, whilst others are purposely designed as non-vocational open-ended courses which provide students with a 'taste' of a wide variety of skills and knowledge which is useful for those who are finding it difficult to make up their minds about the type of career they wish to take up. Most full-time courses are of one year's duration, some are lead-in courses that may be followed up with a second and subsequent years of study, and a few are for less than one year in duration.

If you are interested in taking a full-time course when you leave school keep your eye on the press as most education authorities advertise their courses in local newspapers. Alternatively, ask your school careers teacher to let you know about the courses that are available in your area or, if the opportunity arises, attend a careers convention where college staff are likely to be present who will be willing to give you details of courses that are being offered at their college. If, after having read the literature and talking to college staff, you feel you are interested in a particular college course the next step is to obtain an application form from the college which you must complete and return. The information usually required by a college includes your personal details, the schools you have attended including your present one, details of any examinations you have passed or for which you intend to enter, and your hobbies and interests. You will most likely be called for an interview which will give you an opportunity of meeting one or more members of the

81

college staff and a further opportunity of seeing the college at which you hope to study. A head teacher's report on your subjects of study, your ability and aptitudes, your attainments and conduct is usually obtained by the college which is useful to the staff to assess your suitability for the course for which you have applied.

The college interviewer normally starts the conversation with an explanation of the course and gives details of its duration, content, dates and times of attendance, the amount of course time spent in workshops and laboratories, and gives an idea of the things you would have to supply yourself, such as protective clothing, drawing instruments and stationery. Matters relating to enrolment fees and student grants may also be discussed during the interview. The interviewer expects you to do your share of talking and asking as this gives him a chance to assess your interest and current knowledge on matter relevant to the course.

Block release courses

Block release courses are different from full-time courses or day release courses by their pattern of attendance. A block release student is normally employed by a company and released to the college for block periods of study which are interspersed with periods in his company whereby he receives education and industrial training and experience in alternating phases thereby obtaining a good 'mix' of theoretical learning and practical experience. The block periods or phases in college vary depending upon the particular college and type of course but a six weeks college and six weeks industry cycle is a fairly typical example.

Sandwich courses

Another type of course which is available in some colleges is the sandwich course which often leads to the award of a college diploma on completion. These courses, sometimes termed as courses for high flyers, are designed to cover two or three years duration and are structured from the beginning to give a student preparation for the higher jobs in road transport management and engineering. As there are only a few road transport companies who are willing to release employees for these courses the majority of students who actually take on the courses are college-based and not company-based or sponsored. You will no doubt already have thought about the financial implications of these courses: Who keeps a student whilst taking the course? Who pays the course fee? Who is there who may be willing to sponsor or supply a financial grant? Some cynics would go as far as to say that these courses are only for bosses' sons whose fathers are willing to pay the high course fees, and overseas students who have rich governments to support them! Sandwich courses are designed, not unlike block release courses, with spells which allow time to be spent in industry where some practical experience and training can be obtained. The minimum entry requirements for a sandwich course are usually in the order of three GCE O level passes which include mathematics and another suitable science subject so that a slightly more academic and broader-based curriculum can be studied. Most colleges claim that their sandwich diploma courses have a higher academic standard than the more conventional courses that lead to a craft or technician, or business studies qualification and most of the course examinations lead to part or full exemption for the educational requirements for membership of a professional body.

Integrated training courses

These courses consist of a combination of further education and industrial training and operate on a block release pattern whereby each student alternates between his company and his college with six weeks block training periods in college being fairly common. During the period in college a student attends lectures for his further education studies which cover a similar range of subjects to those students who attend day release courses, but approximately two-thirds of his time spent in college is devoted to approved practical training in the college workshops where skills training is received. Colleges that offer integrated courses have approval of the relevant industrial training board and have to be adequately staffed and equipped to be able to provide training in accordance with a training programme which has been agreed with the training board and the employers of the students. The courses are planned to provide progressive training for young people and may extend over a period of three or four years thereby matching the development of the apprentice or trainee from his first year of training to the completion of his apprenticeship or training period.

Courses for specific careers

Having explained about the different patterns of courses in colleges we can now look at more of the detail included in the courses which are designed to relate to specific careers. It is worth remembering that the choice of course is not always made entirely by the young person, as his employer also likes to have a say in the type of course his employee is taking up—after all, the employer is going to pay a wage to the young person whilst he attends a course and quite rightly wants to be involved in the choice and decision.

Craftsmen and technicians

The range of courses for craftsmen and technicians that will be offered to you depends on the particular college you are interested in attending but at the best, and provided you have a job, will consist of day release courses and block release courses for craftsmen and technicians, and integrated courses in both these areas. Day release courses are very popular and are pursued by many young apprentice craftsmen. The chart on the facing page shows how a student can progress on a college course by starting at First Year level at the age of 16 and studying over a four-year period, for which he will be awarded Parts 1, 2 and 3 certificates by the City and Guilds of London Institute if successful in his examinations. Though the course chart shown is that for a heavy vehicle mechanic, progress for other apprentice craftsmen follows a similar pattern, most courses basically being of four years duration and designed to coincide with a four year apprenticeship. The subjects studied on these courses are technology, associated studies and liberal studies. The subject 'technology' includes the technical aspects of the course these being descriptions, functions, defects and remedies of the components and units which the apprentice needs to know about to do his job well and properly. The 'associated studies' component of the course includes the related science and mathematics which are support subjects for the technology, and the liberal studies component is divided into complementary and contrasting studies both having a large non-technical content. To give you a clearer idea of how the curriculum is designed we will consider one very small part of the syllabus for a heavy vehicle mechanic—the clutch. During the technology lesson the student will learn about the different types of

84

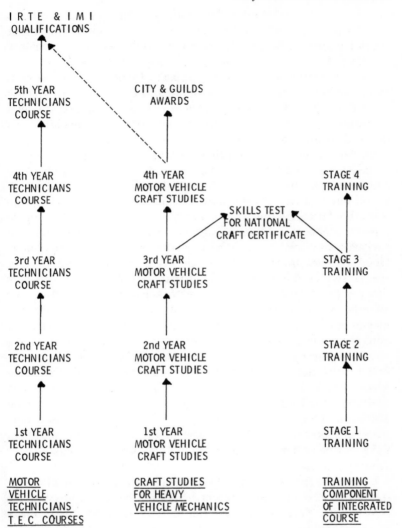

Student progress over a four year course

clutches used in trucks and buses, he will learn how to describe clutch operation and function, and he will learn something about the defects which cause a clutch to fail and the remedies necessary to make it serviceable again. In the associated studies lesson a student will study the scientific aspects of clutches, the material from which its components are made and the reasons why these materials are used, and some calculations will be practised which give students some understanding of the function of the clutch and the ideas behind its design.

Students cover the basic principles of their craft in the first year of the course and delve into the more specialised aspects of technology and science as they progress through the second, third and fourth years. The first year of craft studies is fairly common to most of the specialised trades within a particular group, such as those for vehicle repair craftsmen and because of this there may well be students of various craft disciplines all together in the first year of a craft course. Once students progress to the second year, however, and begin to specialise they split up into courses that are tailor-made to provide them with the specific knowledge to learn their craft. Students attending a first year motor vehicle craft studies course, for example, may be apprentice light vehicle mechanics, heavy vehicle mechanics, auto-electricians, partsmen or body repairers. There is of course much common ground to be covered by all these specialists in the first year of their studies and the overlapping of the subject matter across the various craft boundaries is a good thing as each specialist craftsman needs to know something about his colleagues' job to be able to co-operate in the workshop. A further sub-division may occur at a later stage in courses, an example of this being the split of the heavy vehicle mechanics into heavy goods vehicle and passenger vehicle mechanics.

Unlike the first, second and third years of a craft studies course, the fourth year may be different by taking the form of a modular type course. This means that students may enrol for one or more specialised subjects depending upon their specialised job and individual interest. It is customary to enrol for three modules if the type of attendance is day release and a separate examination is sat at the end of the course of study for each module as each is independent of the other. This is a different system from that which exists in the earlier years of study, where courses are known as grouped courses, and students are expected to sit the two or three examinations at the end of each year of the course. It is necessary to pass in each of the component parts of the examination to qualify for the award of a certificate.

To proceed further with the example already selected, that of the heavy vehicle mechanic, it would be a normal progression at fourth year level to take up the subjects of 'compression ignition engines', 'fuel injection equipment for compression ignition engines' and 'air braking systems for heavy vehicles'.

Although a four-year course is average for most aprentice craftsmen there are a few young people who feel they would like to carry on with their studies even though they may have completed their apprenticeships and even though, in some cases, further day release may not be allowed. There are a number of alternatives that a young person may consider after completing a craft course, one possibility being to bridge across to a professional course, the content of such courses is explained on page 85.

Integrated training courses for craft students

Integrated courses have already been explained in this book and we are now going to take a deeper look at these courses as they affect the training of apprentice craftsmen. It is important to realise that all colleges do not offer integrated courses. One reason being that some of the companies in a college catchment area do not wish to support such courses. For another reason some colleges themselves do not wish to offer the courses because they do not have sufficient resources to cope with the large practical training component of the course, or the colleges who do wish to offer courses cannot obtain approval from the respective training board to offer them.

As already stated, further education and industrial training are two very different things and an integrated course is designed to combine and mix (integrate) the two in such a way as to make up a viable, efficient and worthwhile course with benefits to the employers and the students alike. (See chart below) The further education component of the courses is very similar to the day release further education courses which have already been described. The training component, however, which is the larger part of an integrated course is practically biased and compares more closely with the practical training that a day-release student would receive with his company. Colleges follow a programme of training that is carefully prepared

Integrated training courses

FURTHER EDUCATION COMPONENT		
Heavy Vehicle Technology	Associated Studies	Liberal Studies
6	4	2
TOTAL 12 Hours / week		

TRAINING COMPONENT		
Motor Vehicle Workshop	Engineering Machine Shop	Welding Shop
16	$3\frac{1}{2}$	$3\frac{1}{2}$
TOTAL 23 Hours / week		

PATTERN OF A TYPICAL INTEGRATED TRAINING COURSE
FOR A FIRST-YEAR (STAGE 1) HEAVY VEHICLE MECHANIC

to match with the further education in the course, and the two components provide a sound basis on which students can progressively acquire technical knowledge and practical skills. The training for the acquisition of practical skills and techniques in mainly carried out in college workshops which are adequately staffed and equipped with vehicles, components, tools and equipment for use by students.

A college's training facilities are selected to provide students with a wide variety of experience on different makes of vehicles and vehicle components, and a good selection of tools and equipment is available for use by students so that a broad based (horizontal) training is received with little emphasis being placed on 'product knowledge'. Liaison with employers is maintained by college staff whilst students are pursuing integrated courses, and regular progress reports are despatched to employers informing them of the particular skills which have been taught to their employees and the standard of attainment reached by each student in the skill areas. Employers also take advantage of the advisory committee meetings, which are held regularly in colleges, to ask about the training that is being given to their employees. In addition to the college reports that are forwarded to employers at regular intervals during the training periods each student holds a record book which is completed progressively by the college staff and his employer as he proceeds with the course.

Students who are placed on integrated courses are not 'thrown in at the deep end' when carrying out practical training but are given instruction under carefully controlled and regulated conditions. It would of course be a nonsense to allow a student to proceed with a practical task in a workshop without first giving him an explanation of the way to tackle the task, and a demonstration of how to go about the particular task. So each task is broken down into four elements—explanation, demonstration, participation and controlled experience—and every stage is passed through by the individual student as he learns the skills, techniques and job knowledge of each task as he works towards the fixed objectives and the standards that are acceptable by employers. Because of the limited amount of time that is at the disposal of students during their course some of the latter two elements, participation and controlled experience need to be continued and practised after the student has completed his task at college and are continued when they return to their company.

It is impossible in a book of this length to give a number of examples of tasks that are tackled by students on integrated courses but, to give you some idea of the way the courses are designed, we will look again at the 'clutch' topic which has already been selected as a topic for a day-release course. During the training component of an integrated course the vehicle clutch would be explained to students with the course aim strongly emphasised. If the aim was, say, to remove and replace a clutch in a heavy goods vehicle the explanation would cover the systematic procedure to be used to go about the task which would include any key points related to safety. The college lecturer would then demonstrate the way to go about the task which may be done with the use of a vehicle or a purpose built rig, the latter having the advantage of being more accessible for the lecturer who may be imparting instructions to as many as twelve students. Following the demonstration of how the task should be tackled the students are then allocated a vehicle or a rig and proceed with the participative part of their training. Most of the students' time is taken up by participating and this is the area of training where skills are acquired and techniques are learned and perfected. During these three elements of training the theoretical knowledge of clutches, which has been learned in the further education component of the course, is being assimilated and consolidated by the student. Each year of an integrated course is usually regarded as a 'stage' (see chart page 85) and there are normally three stages which correspond with the first three years of a young person's apprenticeship.

Stage one, the first year, is a general introduction to the specialised training which follows in the later stages and, because of its large basic common content, is suitable for first-year heavy goods mechanics,

PSV fitters, light vehicle mechanics auto-electricians and partsmen. When students progress to Stages Two and Three, (second and third years), they follow a programme specially written for their particular needs, and separate courses are necessary for the various specialists. Because of this specialisation it may mean that some students have to change their college after the Stage One course and attend wherever the course they need is available.

Following on from the three stages of technical training is a fourth stage which is becoming more popular as far as off-the-job courses are concerned. Though the fourth stage or fourth year may seem to be a long way off to a young person who is just embarking on a career, it will eventually arrive and it is therefore better to be prepared for it. In addition to the controlled experience which is gained by fourth year apprentices in their final year of training there are several other topics that may be included in their training schemes which help to round off their experience and skills. These topics include training for carrying out pre-Department of Transport vehicle inspections, fault diagnosis, familiarisation of company departments, other than the one in which the apprentice normally works, and job instruction.

The latter topic, *job instruction,* differs from the type of training received during the first three stages as it is aimed at final and subsequent year students who are to take on additional skills and responsibilities for the purpose of training the younger apprentices in their companies in an on-the-job situation. Job instruction courses include training to impart skills and knowledge to younger apprentices who are new to the industry. The overall object being to improve standards of apprentice training throughout the road transport industry. The courses include instructions and practice with the use of training aids, and course members are given tips on how to improve communications between themselves and the young people they are to train. There is also plenty of practice in carrying out job demonstrations in the presence of the other course members on whom he can try out his question and answer techniques. An instructor is expected to stress the key points of a demonstration and these include the safety points which must be brought in to all demonstrations. Course members are taught how to prepare for their demonstrations so that everything runs smoothly when they are actually doing them. There is often a tendency to assume that an instructor's job is all too easy—until it is tried—and it is only when people attempt to give job instructions that they begin to appreciate what is involved.

So the four years of integrated training start with a broad basic training, followed by two further years of specialised training, and concluding with a final year of consolidation by obtaining controlled experience and further specialised training such as that obtained from attending a job instructor's course. In all, integrated courses provide young people with a sound practical training and the further education to make a success of a future career in the road transport industry. These courses are well worth taking up if you are given the opportunity.

Courses for technicians

Most colleges offer courses for technicians as well as for craftsmen and as there is often some confusion about the differences between these two types of engineer in the road transport industry we will look at the role of the technician and compare the differences between him and the craftsman. Starting with the courses available for technicians in colleges it must be understood at the outset that there are some differences and you should think carefully if you are faced with a choice between enrolling for a technician or a craft studies course.

The first thing you should look into is the course content, as the syllabus subject matter is treated in greater depth than in the craft courses and a more mathematical and scientific approach is required by students. The main purpose of technician education is to provide a young person with a broad technical knowledge on to which he can build more specialised knowledge and skills of either a technical or managerial nature. This course is to equip him with the essential tools to tackle some of the highly specialised jobs within his industry. A skilled technician is expected to be able to diagnose faults in a vehicle in addition to being able to repair and rectify them, and he must have the know-how to analyse the performance of a vehicle after repair or modification has been carried out. Many technicians are employed as vehicle testers, reception engineers, and foremen. Others specialise after completing their courses in supervisory studies and management as transport engineers and managers. Technician and management qualifications, together with experience and responsibility in the road transport industry, qualify young people for membership of a professional body and this type of high level qualification is often sought by those who wish to rise to the top in the transport world.

Technician courses are, therefore, as you would no doubt expect, fuller than craft courses and the pace of technician courses is much quicker. You not only have to work harder but also you have to work for longer as a typical college day for a day release technician's course would consist of about eight hours of intensive classroom and laboratory activity with an additional evening attendance making a total of ten hours a week at college. In addition to college work there is a good deal more to do at home than you would have to do if you were attending a craft course. All this needs careful thought before you finally decide. Your company may also want to know about your decision on the course you have selected and may wish to guide you as to the type of course they think is most suitable. One disappointing point about taking on a technician's course, which some young people discover after completing a course, is that their company cannot offer them a job which is commensurate with their qualification. This sometimes leads to frustration and loss of interest. When occasionally this does happen, it is not always the company that is to blame for the situation as some companies are so limited in size, staffing or structure that they are not able to offer a more senior job to a newly qualified young person. This is sometimes the reason why some employers do not wish their new apprentices to embark on a technician course. This point is worth discussing with a prospective employer at your interview or with your employer if you have just started a job.

Many technicians are employed in the truck and bus industry but their individual roles depend, to a large extent, on the size, structure and nature of the business. In a small repair garage for example, the foreman may be educated to technician level and a large proportion of his time in the company may be devoted to fault diagnosis on vehicles and documentation. Some of his responsibility is to delegate some of the workshop jobs to the craftsmen under his control who may call on the foremen from time to time to help them sort out a snag job which they cannot sort out for themselves. This sort of situation gives the foreman an opportunity to practise his technician knowledge and skills as he lends a helping hand. This example shows the differences between the technician and the craftsman, the former having the authority to delegate jobs which is part of his supervisory function and the ability to demonstrate a higher technical ability which is part of his technician function.

Technician courses in colleges usually span over a period of five years (see chart page 85) and there is a possibility of one or two further years for those people who wish to take on courses for the examination requirements of the professional bodies. This is much longer than the four year span which is normal for a craftsman to complete his course and should also be thought about before embarking on a technician course.

Courses for supervisors and managers

It is shown in the chart on page 85 that a young person can progress via craft and technician courses to courses of a more advanced nature in supervision and management. In the early days in road transport, firemen, transport engineers and managers were trained on-the-job by their superiors and remained essentially practical people at their jobs. Transport engineers, for example, would have spent a lifetime dealing with the practical intricacies of vehicle maintenance, and managers would have devoted a considerable portion of their working lives to establishing and maintaining contacts with customers for whom their vehicles were carrying, with relatively little of their time having to be devoted to the involvement in administrative, management and clerical duties that are essential today.

But, today, foremen and managers have no alternative but to spend a considerable amount of their time on non-practical duties and their further education and training is designed to prepare them in their early years for the type of work that they are likely to take on later in their careers. There is an enormous amount of document work which includes form filling for such issues as vehicle licensing, vehicle inspection schedules, preparation and application for D o T vehicle tests, accident reports, vehicle maintenance schedules, staff training programmes, time and job records from staff, load handling and delivery notes. All this needs some time and attention from the transport engineer and the manager. A few young people become disillusioned shortly after taking up a career in road transport when they discover that they may eventually have to face up to leaving the nuts and bolts (a mechanic's job) or abandoning the steering wheel (a driver's job) in order to advance towards the higher management jobs in the industry.

Courses in supervision and management are designed to prepare young people for the higher jobs, and effectively graft on to a student's already gained technical or commercial experience another layer of knowledge and skill in the principles and rudiments of supervision and management as preparation for the higher jobs. Some experienced engineers and managers argue that a person can only become efficient in management by practising management and this argument is no doubt true. However, the theoretical knowledge and skills acquired by a young person, before he becomes a manager or engineer, give him some insight into the roles of people in the higher jobs.

The City and Guilds of London Institute

As so many young people take college courses which lead to a City and Guilds qualification and, as there are so few people who know much about this Institute, it is worth taking a close look at it and its standing in relation to the truck and bus industry.

The City and Guilds was established in 1878 by the Corporation of the City of London and some of the City Livery Companies 'the Guilds'. It was incorporated by Royal Charter in 1900. It has recently celebrated its centenary year and is continuing to gain in status as a professional institute with a world-wide reputation. In 1977 the City and Guilds assessed a record number of candidates this being in excess of 400 000 and there are some five million holders of City and Guilds qualifications throughout the world.

The City and Guilds works in close collaboration with a number of other national and regional bodies, two of these being the North West Regional Advisory Council for Further Education which incorporates the Union of Lancashire and Cheshire Institutes, and the East Midland Educational Union, to develop education and training. Its committees consist of many highly qualified and experienced people from industry and commerce, the education service, Government departments and so on, who work with local government officials to establish national standards of technical knowledge and skills to meet the needs of a wide range of industries which include the truck and bus industry. A candidate's performance in relation to these standards is measured by examinations and tests that are administered by the City and Guilds.

How can I progress for a City and Guilds award?
The chart on the facing page shows how a young person can progress

from school leaving age and first employment to professional status by achieving certification awarded by the City and Guilds.

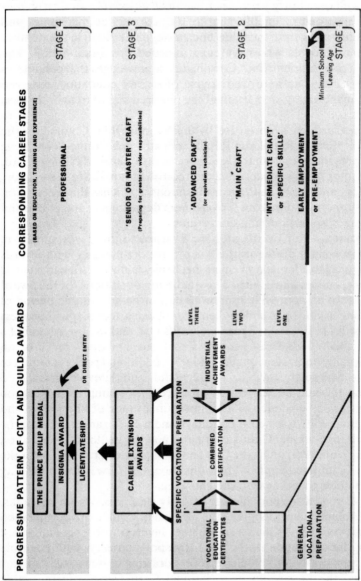

Reproduced by kind permission of the City and Guilds of London Institute

95

The National Craft Certificate

It is well over thirty years since the first National Craft Certificates were awarded to qualified motor vehicle service mechanics and from this early time there has been a steady increase in the number of young people who have been awarded this qualification. The award of a National Craft Certificate acknowledges that candidates have pursued an approved course of further education, received practical training, and attained the required standard in both these areas.

The Certificate is awarded by the National Joint Council for the Motor Vehicle Retail and Repair Industry, the Council consisting of representatives from the Road Transport Industry Training Board, the Motor Agents Association, the Scottish Motor Trade Association, the City and Guilds, and the trade unions, and it has the recognition and support of numerous Government departments and public and private corporations and companies.

National Craft Certificates are awarded to those who qualify in their specialised area in the road transport industry with awards being available for heavy vehicle mechanics, auto-electricians, vehicle body repairers and others. The qualifying conditions for the award consist of an approved apprenticeship or an acceptable period of training having been undertaken by applicants, together with success in the RTITB's Stage 3 practical skills test, and the possession of a City and Guilds Craft Studies Certificate at Part 2 level, or an acceptable equivalent qualification. An additional pocket certificate is also awarded by the NJC, to successful candidates which is a good idea as this may be carried and produced, for example when at a job interview, as evidence of attainment in a range of knowledge and practical skills assessed at national standards. Arrangements for the awards of National Craft Certificates and the issuing of application forms is undertaken by the City and Guilds who act as agents for the NJC. Completed application forms should be forwarded to the City and Guilds together with the entry fee.

The road transport industry rightly deserves, within its ranks, well trained young people of the high calibre which this certification helps produce. As higher and higher levels of professionalism are being insisted upon in the road transport industry, with licensing and registration of vehicle repairers drawing closer to becoming a reality, the possession of a National Craft Certificate by young people is almost certain to be of benefit to them in their future careers. There are not many other skilled trades that can boast of a national qualification that recognises their skills and knowledge as does the National Craft Certificate which is awarded to those in the road transport industry.

The Technician Education Council (TEC) and the Business Education Council (BEC)

The Technician Education Council was set up by a former Secretary of State for Education and Science following the Hazelgrave Report in 1969 on the future of technician courses and examinations. Technician education is playing an increasing role in the road transport industry. Technicians occupy jobs in the truck and bus industry that fall between crafstmen on the one hand and technologists on the other. In addition to providing certification for craftsmen, the City and Guilds, together with a number of regional examining boards, were also responsible for the certification of technicians prior to the setting up of TEC but this role is presently being phased out by City and Guilds as the TEC becomes established. Courses that are offered in colleges are designed and structured to educate students for their specialised fields so as to enable them to exercise technical judgement in their jobs by their possession of a sound understanding of the general principles involved in their work. The technician, by virtue of his education and training, is different from a craftsman in the road transport industry. He is expected to be able to exercise judgement in a diagnostic sense and an appraisal sense, the former on work in which he may be directly involved and the latter when supervising others.

Most TEC courses that are taken by young people in the truck and bus industry consist of a programme of 'units' (see table overleaf) which are devised and supplied by the TEC to colleges. A unit is defined as a 'self-contained and significant component of a programme which will be separately assessed and, if successfully completed, count for credit towards a student's award'. The TEC award Certificates, Higher Certificates, Diplomas and Higher Diplomas to students who have satisfactorily completed a course which may be taken by day release, block release or full-time study.

The modular scheme which contains a wide choice of units in the TEC programmes gives opportunities for both greater flexibility and economy for the education of technicians than has ever existed

97

Level I (1st year)	Engine technology	Vehicle technology	
Level II (2nd year)	Engine technology	Vehicle technology	Engine draw (½ unit
Level III (3rd year)	Petrol or diesel engine technology	Steering, brakes, suspension	Engine draw (½ u

Programme of a typical three-year day release motor vehicle technician's course which leads to the award of a TEC Certificate. Each study unit is of two hours' duration making a total of ten hours a week attendance for a period of three years. It is possible to continue after this course for study leading to the award of a Higher TEC Certificate

before. Within limits the TEC programmes can be tailored to meet the requirements of truck and bus operators, thereby providing a sound relevant educational base on which their young people can build.

The development of the BEC courses in colleges is taking a similar pattern to the development of the TEC courses, but a large number of professional bodies have been involved with the establishment of standards and the determination of curricula. It is almost certain that young people who are attending college courses in the future will, in most cases, be taking BEC courses to qualify themselves for jobs as traffic clerks and transport managers in the road transport industry.

Professional qualifications

Those letters after a person's name represent his professional qualifications. You may have noticed on printed letter headings that abbreviations (letters) are sometimes given after the principal's or the writer's name. In some cases these letters indicate that the person holds a university degree, for example, a BA or a BSc, or they may indicate that he is a Justice of the Peace by the letters JP but, in the truck and bus industry, you are more likely to see abbreviations that indicate membership of a professional body to

:s	Science and Report writing	General and Communication studies	
Maths ½ unit)	Science and Report writing	Workshop processes and materials (½ unit)	General and Communication studies (½ unit)
Electrical systems	Science and Report writing		General and Communication studies (½ unit)

which the holder belongs. He may, in fact, be a member of more than one professional institute and display a string of letters after his name.

Possession of a professional qualification is highly desirable for those in, or aspiring to, the higher jobs in the truck and bus industry and many young people already in this industry are aiming at becoming a member of an appropriate professional body. Professional institutes and associations hold a high status within the industry they represent and membership of an institute can make advice, information, news, friendship and involvement possible for individual members.

Entry into a professional body is not as easy as joining a Christmas club. It is not simply a matter of filling in a card with a few personal details and paying a joining fee. All applicants for membership of professional bodies have to meet strict entry requirements which include success in examinations, sound industrial experience, good personal character, and, in the case of application to the higher grades of membership, responsibility in the industry. An application for membership also requires the backing of two or more members of the professional body who act as sponsors and vouch that the applicant's statements about himself that are listed on his application are true.

The Institute of Road Transport Engineers

This is a professional body whose basic aims are to improve the technical, commercial and general skill, knowledge and competence of all whose occupation or vocation is the operation of road vehicles used for transporting goods, passengers and equipment. Included in the Institute's further aims is the encouragement and training of young people to acquire theoretical and practical qualifications and raise the professional standard of all the Institute's members. Many young people who are studying to become road transport engineers and managers take further studies at the end of their technical studies (see page 85) in supervisory and managerial subjects which include road transport law and the Certificate of Professional Competence requirements. Success in these studies qualifies young people for the academic requirements demanded by the Institute for membership and, when coupled with practical experience and responsibility, leads to the much coveted higher grades of Institute membership.

The Institute of the Motor Industry

This is a professional body which embraces every aspect of the motor industry including the heavy vehicle sector. The Institute sets high standards for membership and has a comprehensive system of examinations which are sat annually by hundreds of young people who are studying with a view towards becoming members of this body.

The IMI is now sixty years old and was founded by a few far-sighted motor traders and engineers who then saw the need for nationally organised standards of education and training for young people who are to enter the vehicle repair industry. Since those early days many thousands of young people have qualified as craftsmen and technicians as a result of this far-sightedness of those early pioneers. One of the reasons why the IMI and those involved with it, are respected so highly in the motor industry today is the importance it attaches to its Code of Conduct and, if you think about joining the IMI on some future occasion, you must observe this Code in all your professional dealings.

Chartered Institute of Transport

This professional body is mainly for those people in the truck and bus industry who are involved in the transport and traffic side.

Young people who are about to enter the truck and bus industry and those who have just entered it are advised to find out about the many activities of the CIT as it is one of the most sought after qualifications in transport. The minimum age for joining is seventeen, and the studentship of the CIT is open to those engaged, or intending to become engaged, in or in connection with transport.

100

Some of the subjects in the qualifying examinations for CIT membership are transport economics, management and control of transport, manpower and industrial relations. If you are considering a career in this side of road transport then these are some of the subjects you will need to study.

Institute of Traffic Administration

Many experienced people in road transport who are in top jobs hold an IoTA qualification. The Institute has devised an education and examination scheme suitable for young people who are just starting to make a career in this industry which provides a standard of education in subjects on which a practical career in transport and traffic administration can be developed.

Courses may be taken by students at most of the colleges in the UK which lead up to the Institute's examinations in subjects which include the development of modern transport, transport operations and commercial practice. At a more advanced level further subjects may be taken which are necessary for people who wish to apply for associate membership of the Institute. These include statistics, principles of law, economics, transport management and administration, finance and accounting. The Institute also offers a diploma in traffic administration which may be awarded to members holding GCE O levels in English and mathematics and who write a thesis on the subject of traffic administration. You can see for yourself that those GCE certificates that have been mentioned in this book are more than likely to be of use to you at a later stage in your career. If you do not possess GCEs or their equivalents and you are not in the process of taking any, then it is worth bearing in mind that it is possible to take these at a college sometime in the future.

The Institute provides advice to young people, including school leavers, in road transport careers and it is willing to supply information to young people who are thinking about making road transport their career.

Certificate of Professional Competence (CPC)

The licensing laws for people who operate goods vehicles are very stringent and it is necessary for people to qualify on the grounds of professional competence to obtain an Operators' Licence to run goods vehicles in the road haulage sector of the industry. Young people who hope to aspire to the higher positions in transport management need therefore to study the topics of road safety, traffic regulations, drivers' hours, safe loading, law, taxation, costing, and a number of other subjects, to prepare themselves for an examination which must be passed to obtain a CPC. Courses for preparation for the examinations are offered by colleges, correspondence schools, Motecs, and a number of other training centres, and the examinations are set from Royal Society of Arts syllabuses, the latter being the body which issues the Certificates to successful candidates.

Driver training for trucking

Most of the road haulage companies and the fleet operators pay a levy to their industrial training board which entitles them to receive, in return, financial grants for the purpose of training their employees as drivers. Some of the large companies have their own driver training schools, other companies group themselves into training associations, and others use the training centres operated by the Road Transport Industry Training Board or the private training schools in their locality for training drivers. A course of instruction, together with the fee for an HGV driving test, is costly and, because of this, very few young people embark on a course for HGV training unless employed by a company who will foot the bill.

Today a driver must be very knowledgeable about his job, and a great deal of professionalism enters into his work. Basically, all drivers need to understand that there are regulations with which they must comply and these are brought to the notice of all trainee drivers during their training period. The overriding consideration which must be borne in mind by all drivers, HGV and PSV alike, is safety to the public. Drivers must at all times comply with the Law, after all, a driver's job depends on him having and keeping his licence to drive. At the end of a driver training period a trainee is entered for his test. The HGV Driving Test lasts about two hours and consists of manoeuvering a vehicle in a confined space, driving over a twenty-five mile route on a mixture of rural and urban roads in varying traffic densities, and the testing of the trainee's knowledge of the Highway Code, and components that affect the safe operation and function of the vehicle. Good HGV drivers are experienced in a wide range of skills which include the ability to follow planned routes quickly and accurately, estimate the height of low bridges, sheet and rope loads securely, know how to deal with a high-jacking situation, and know how to tackle vehicle breakdown situations when away from base. The ability to use intelligently a vehicle's instrument panel can also be of great benefit to a driver and his company, as dashboard instruments, when used properly, can often give an indication of a defect that is developing in a vehicle component and a good driver will take action immediately he is warned that something is not quite right.

In addition to all the general training that a driver needs there is usually some special training that is necessary for him to do in his particular job safely and efficiently. An example of this is the tanker driver. It has been known for tankers to break down, crash, collide or go out of control and burst into flames. This sounds dramatic but it emphasises the need for special training for drivers of tankers as the risk of fire, explosion, spillage, and escape of noxious gases can never be completely ruled out, no matter how much care is taken. Tanker companies therefore provide training for inexperienced personnel so that they are able to tackle their work competently and safely. Driver training may include visits to chemical works where the effects of various chemicals can be practically demonstrated and drivers can be given instructions on how to cope with a leak or a spillage when on the road. Drivers are instructed on the operation of the various types of fire extinguisher and one or more is usually carried on a vehicle which may be used if an occasion arises. Drivers are also issued with a safety clothing kit comprising of a helmet, goggles, or an eye shield, a bottle of eye-wash, a PVC boilersuit, gloves and rubber boots which may be used when necessary. In some cases breathing apparatus is carried on vehicles for use by the driver if needed.

HGV driver training for young people

Some young people think that the age of eighteen will never arrive for them and, as this is the age when a person is normally eligible to take a Heavy Goods Vehicle driving licence, are put off the idea of taking up driving as a career.

A new scheme has therefore been recently introduced which should help to solve this problem for some young people. The scheme is drawn up by the National Joint Training Committee for Young HGV Drivers in the Road Goods Transport Industry, the Committee consisting of representatives from the Department of

Transport, the Road Transport Industry Training Board, the Road Haulage Association, the Freight Transport Association, the Training Services Agency and the trade unions. The scheme is based on a progressive programme of training and related further education which enables a school leaver at the age of 16 to embark on a career which will ultimately qualify him to become a professional driver.

The first year of training between the age of 16 and 17 may be spent in the various departments of a company where experience may be gained in the loading bays, warehouses, goods yards and so on, and different experience may be obtained by working as a driver's mate which makes a useful and enlightening start into the world of trucking. On reaching the age of 17 the young person may, after receiving some tuition, take a driving test for an ordinary driving licence which will enable him to drive light goods vehicles which do not exceed 3.5 tonnes maximum weight when driving at 17 and a maximum of 7.5 tonnes when he is 18. The new scheme enables a young person employed with a registered company, and pursuing an approved programme of education and training, to progress to a Class 3 HGV licence holder at 18 which enables him to drive four-wheeled goods vehicles on revenue duties for his company. Further to this it is possible to progress in some companies after a twelve-month period of holding a Class 3 licence to a Class 2 licence which enables six and eight wheeled goods vehicles to be driven. After a further twelve-month period as holder of a Class 2 licence, he may progress to a Class 1 licence which enables the holder to drive the heaviest permitted articulated vehicles, provided he is over 21. If under 21 he must be accompanied by an adult driver, even though he may have passed the Class 1 test. There is one important clause in the scheme which does not permit a young person under 21 to drive a Class 1 vehicle unless accompanied by an adult driver.

All companies do not, of course, have a full range of goods vehicles from light vans to heavy articulated trucks which would be necessary to provide the ideal opportunity, as outlined here, but there are however a few. You can no doubt think of several examples of companies in your area which operate a limited range of goods vehicles that are suitable for their particular type of haulage, and these may well be four wheeled rigid box trucks of about 16 tonnes gross weight or short wheel based eight wheeler tippers. In these examples the former trucks would require Class 3 drivers and the latter Class 2 drivers.

Trainee drivers under this scheme are granted their driving licences to drive for their registered employer only and record books are used during the training period to record the trainee's progress. Some of the basic information required by young drivers is obtained whilst following a further education programme which may be based on a day-release or block-release course of approximately one year's duration. The course is examinable, and successful trainees are awarded a certificate after the completion of the course.

Training to be a bus driver

Although most people who take up training for bus driving have an ordinary driving licence, and some have an HGV licence as well, specific instructions are normally required before a PSV driving test is taken. The National Bus Company (NBC) and the Passenger Transport Authorities (PTAs) use training buses which are specially adapted for driver training. These buses are purposely re-designed so that they can easily be identified by other road users and pedestrians by their colours, signs and markers, to avoid confusion with other buses that are in service. Some of these training buses have had a minimum amount of alteration for adaption to driver training vehicles and these can quickly and easily be re-converted and put back into service if required. In some cases the only significant alteration that is made is the removal of the window which separates the driver's cab and the saloon and this can easily be removed and replaced. But other bus companies make more permanent alterations to their vehicles which include the fitting of a special observation seat and a separate brake pedal for the instructor. The training given to bus drivers is not necessarily more intensive that that given to HGV trainee drivers but it is certainly different. A bus driver is trained in such a way that he is always concious of the passengers he is carrying and for whom he is responsible. He is trained to be pleasant to passengers at all times and he is expected, when he goes into service, to offer occasional assistance. He is trained to avoid, or lose, bad habits and maintain a good attitude towards passengers as he is regarded by his company as their public relations man.

Preparation for a PSV Driving Test means, once again, going back to the classroom to listen to experienced instructors who, with the aid of audio and visual equipment, provide trainees with driving theory, details of Highway Code, and ample information on the topics of passenger safety and comfort. A driver of a double-deck bus, for example, must always be aware of his bus height and width. There are a number of tunnels and bridges throughout the country that are too low for a double-deck bus to pass under and there are occasional accidents caused by a driver taking his bus into a tunnel which damages the roof or, in severe cases, tears it off. Similar damage can be caused to a double decker by striking overhanging tree branches.

Bus driver training continues beyond the stage where a driver obtains his PSV licence. In addition, he has to become familiar with the different types of vehicles within his company. Some of the older buses may have manual-change gearboxes, later ones may be fitted with semi-automatic or fully-automatic gear boxes. Many modern buses have rear-mounted engines and these are harder to hear than front-mounted ones. This can give problems when gear changing leading to excessive wear and damage to the vehicle's transmission as well as discomfort to the passengers.

Other aspects of driver training include the reporting procedures to be used for a faulty or damaged vehicle, an accident, or a delay when in service. Instructions are also given in fire precautions and passenger safety in the event of an accident. Before a driver can be placed in service he has to be trained in route familiarisation, stops and terminus procedures, vehicle checking-in procedures and completion of running documents.

Before taking over a bus and driving it out of the garage, or when taking over from a colleague, a driver is usually responsible for carrying out a number of vehicle checks and adjustments which may include a visual examination of the tyres, an inspection of the body for damage and broken components. Other checks and adjustments in the vehicle's cab include the driving seat and the rear view mirrors. The instrument panel should be checked to make sure that the braking system and the electrical components are functioning properly.

A number of buses are one-man-operated (OMO) and the driver of these has also to be trained as a conductor. This aspect of his job consists of the issue of tickets and collection of fares, and an understanding of fare charts, bus passes, clipper cards, dog and parcel carriage, lost property, and the company's rules regarding the carriage and the conduct of passengers.

Special operations

Further training needs to be given to drivers who work on coach operations, long distance travel and private hire work. A certain amount of simple vehicle repair knowledge is given by some companies which includes the use of tools that are needed to change a road wheel if punctured, and the procedure to be followed to 'bleed' a fuel injection pump if the diesel engine is suspected of having an air lock.

Drivers need a good knowledge of motorway services, restaurant locations and some First Aid training. They also have the responsibility for making sure the bus or coach is securely locked up at the end of a journey and is opened up and, if need be, warmed up before setting out on a long journey. Some cleaning and sweeping out is also expected from drivers who are on tour with their vehicle.

Conclusion

I hope that your appetite for a career in road transport will have been whetted after reading this book. It is of course impossible to cover every facet of the truck and bus industry in such a short book but I set out to give a wide spread of information about this industry so that you may judge for yourselves which areas are likely to be of the most interest to you.

Reliability, honesty and enthusiasm are all important personal qualities and employers expect to see these qualities in young people who they take in their companies. Reliability is important to truck and bus operators because of the service they are carrying out for other people, and employers can only meet the requests and demands of others if their own staff are reliable towards them. This means you will be expected to be punctual at work, be willing to do a little extra work after the normal finishing time if asked, and to go about your daily tasks in a pleasant and willing manner. Anyone who constantly grumbles and moans about his work soon becomes a bore to his colleagues as well as to his employers. Reliability will be expected in timekeeping, turning in to work regularly, and in your standards of workmanship. There will be times when you are working alone and your employer will expect you to be trustworthy and loyal during these times.

Conclusion

It is also necessary to strive to be consistent at work. Being constant to the same principles can also increase your employer's confidence in you, as consistency throughout the company can make a big difference to the consistency and continuation of the operations of the company. A worker who goes about his job with alternate phases of enthusiasm and lethargy has less chance of being successful in his career than someone who is a consistent worker—even though he may be consistently mediocre. Your aim should be to strive for a high level of consistency.

Honesty is also required from you. Most people in transport are handling, at some time or other, other people's goods or property and there is sometimes a temptation to be dishonest. Employers take a serious view of staff who are dishonest and not trustworthy as customers or passengers can be lost or business can suffer as a result of this. It is therefore important that you resist the temptation to cheat or steal at work, and if you damage or break anything that belongs to your employer then admit to him that it is your fault, apologise, and try not to let the same thing happen again.

It will be hard to be consistent about maintaining your enthusiasm all the time you are working but at least you can try. If, for example, you become a driver and get wet through on a rainy day whilst loading your vehicle, or you become a mechanic and injure your thumb whilst using a hammer, your enthusiasm may in the short term wane but if you are sufficiently dedicated to your career your interest and enthusiasm will soon pick up again. One advantage of working with trucks and buses is that every day is a little different and there is far less monotony than there is in many other jobs. So, provided you are sufficiently dedicated to your career, you will have a good opportunity of being successful and rising in the world of trucks and buses to the level that your full potential will allow. Don't forget to try to do your best at all times even though your career will have its ups and downs, be willing to listen and learn, ask questions when you want to know about things, continue with your studies and try to improve your theoretical qualifications, read books and magazines on transport topics, watch television and listen to the radio when trucks and buses are being talked about, and don't be afraid to read your local and national newspapers to broaden your knowledge of the truck and bus industry.

Finally, allow me to take this opportunity of wishing you well with your career with trucks and buses if you have now decided that this

108

is the area where your future career lies. Admittedly it may at times be challenging but the interest that you will have in your work will far outweigh any short term set backs that may arise.

Some useful names and addresses

Amalgamated Union of Engineering Workers (Engineers Section)
110 Peckham Road, London, SE15 5EL

British Association of Removers
279 Gray's Inn Road, London, WC1X 8SY

British Road Services
Northway House, High Road, Whetstone, London, N20 9ND

Chartered Institute of Transport
80 Portland Place, London, W1N 4DP

City and Guilds of London Institute
76 Portland Place, London, W1N 4AA

Commercial Motor IPC Transport Press
Quadrant House, The Quadrant, Sutton, Surrey, SM2 5AS

Department of Transport
Marsham Street, London, SW1

Freight Transport Association
Hermes House, St John's Road, Tunbridge Wells, Kent, TN4 9UZ

Institute of The Motor Industry
Fanshaws, Brickenden, Hertford, SG13 8PG

Institute of Road Transport Engineers
1 Cromwell Place, Kensington, London, SW7 2JF

Institute of Traffic Administration
8 Cumberland Place, Southampton, SO1 2BH

Some useful names and addresses

MOTECS

These are situated at High Ercall in Shropshire and at Livingstone in Scotland.

For details of courses available write to Course Bookings at the Wembley address of RTITB given below

Motor Transport IPC Transport Press
Quadrant House, The Quadrant, Sutton, Surrey, SM2 5AS

Ribble Motor Services Ltd
Frenchwood Avenue, Preston, PR1 4LU

Road Haulage Association
22 Upper Woburn Place, London, WC1H OES

Road Transport Industry Training Board
Capitol House, Empire Way, Wembley, Middlesex, HA9 0NG
14, Cathedral Road, Cardiff, CF1 9LJ
7 Buchanan Street, Glasgow, G1 3HL
73 Crown Street, Aberdeen AB1 QES
ITB House, 33 Church Road, Newtown Abbey,
    Belfast, BT36 7LH

Technician Education Council
76 Portland Place, London, W1N 4AA

Transport and General Workers Union
Transport House, Smith Square, London, SW1P 3JB

Truck Magazine
64 West Smithfields, London, EC1

Index

Mechanics Institutes 80
Mechanical reasoning 20
Modules, education 86
MOTECS 37,77
Motorway services 44

National Joint Council 30,31,
 48,71,96
Numbers of vehicles on roads
 22

One-man-operation 106
Operators' licence 43,101
Ordering of parts 36
Overseas countries 45

Parts lists 36
PAYE 71
Pay packet 70
Personality 19
Personnel officer 17
Pioneers 22,100
Platform trucks 41
Power brakes 66
Probationary period 17
Protective clothing 45,72
PSV Certificate of Fitness 53
PSV Driving test 105
PSV licences 53
Purchase of tools 73

Qualifications 18,48

Rear markers 43
Record book 20,88
Records, training 78
Regional examination boards
 94,97

Registration of repairers 96
Reliability 32,107
Road haulage 25,26
Roadworthy vehicles 23

Selection for jobs 17
Semi-trailers 60
Senior citizen travel 52
Single-deck buses 64
Skilled staff 31
Small companies 11
Starting-up engines 55
Statutory deductions 70,71
Stock taking 36
Student travel 52

Tankers 27,41,103
Tests for suitability 20
Tidy appearance 15
Tipper trucks 41
Tools, purchase of 73
Tractor unit 60
Traffic density 54
Transport cafés 44
Transport law 46
Trams 50
Tricks of the trade 68
Trucks, heavy 56,61
Trunk services 26

Units for TEC 97

Vehicle breakdowns 45

Warehouse people 23
Wheels and axles 56